Bars & Brownies

Recipes to make your own gifts

Use these recipes to delight your friends and family. Each recipe includes gift tags for your convenience – just cut them out and personalize!

To decorate jars, cut fabric in 9" diameter circles. Screw down the jar ring to hold fabric in place or hold fabric with a ribbon, raffia, twine, yarn, lace, or string (first secure the fabric with a rubber band before tying). Punch a hole into the corner of the tag and use the ribbon, raffia, twine, yarn, lace, or string to attach the tag to the jar.

These gifts sho
months. If the mix con
used within three month

Printed in the United States of America
by G&R Publishing Co.

Second Edition

Distributed By:

507 Industrial Street
Waverly, IA 50677

ISBN 1-56383-123-6
Item #3003

Brownie Mix

2 1/4 C. sugar
2/3 C. cocoa powder (clean
   inside of jar with a paper
   towel after this layer)
1/2 C. chopped pecans
1 1/4 C. all-purpose flour
1 tsp. baking powder
1 tsp. salt

Layer the ingredients in the order given into a wide-mouth 1-quart canning jar. Pack each layer in place before adding the next ingredient.

Attach a gift tag with the mixing and baking directions.

Brownies

Makes 24 bars

1 jar Brownie Mix
3/4 C. butter or margarine,
    softened
4 eggs, slightly beaten

Preheat the oven to 350°F. In a large bowl, cream the butter and eggs. Add the Brownie Mix and stir until the mixture is well blended. Spread batter into a lightly greased or sprayed 9 x 12 inch pan. Bake for 30 to 35 minutes. Cool in pan. Cut into 2-inch squares.

Brownies
Makes 24 bars

1 jar Brownie Mix
3/4 C. butter or margarine,
  softened

4 eggs, slightly beaten

Preheat the oven to 350°F. In a large bowl, cream the butter and eggs. Add the Brownie Mix and stir until the mixture is well blended. Spread batter into a lightly greased or sprayed 9 x 12 inch pan. Bake for 30 to 35 minutes. Cool in pan. Cut into 2-inch squares.

Brownies
Makes 24 bars

1 jar Brownie Mix
3/4 C. butter or margarine,
  softened

4 eggs, slightly beaten

Preheat the oven to 350°F. In a large bowl, cream the butter and eggs. Add the Brownie Mix and stir until the mixture is well blended. Spread batter into a lightly greased or sprayed 9 x 12 inch pan. Bake for 30 to 35 minutes. Cool in pan. Cut into 2-inch squares.

Brownies
Makes 24 bars

1 jar Brownie Mix
3/4 C. butter or margarine,
  softened

4 eggs, slightly beaten

Preheat the oven to 350°F. In a large bowl, cream the butter and eggs. Add the Brownie Mix and stir until the mixture is well blended. Spread batter into a lightly greased or sprayed 9 x 12 inch pan. Bake for 30 to 35 minutes. Cool in pan. Cut into 2-inch squares.

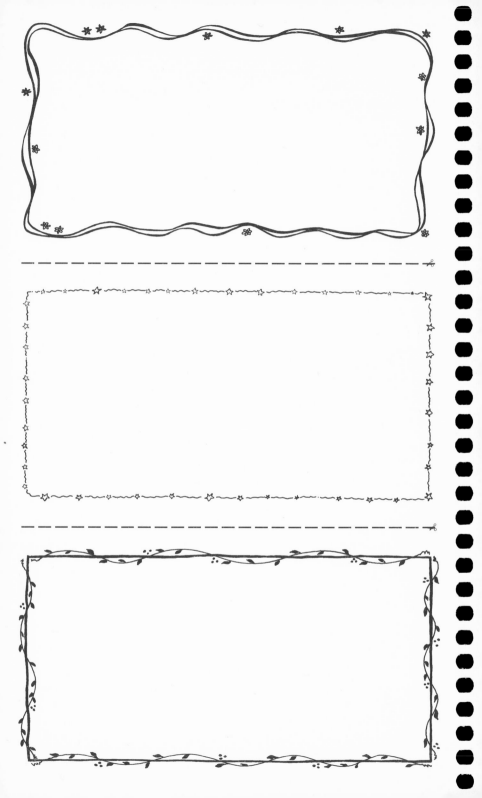

Brownies
Makes 24 bars

1 jar Brownie Mix

4 eggs, slightly beaten

3/4 C. butter or margarine,
softened

Preheat the oven to 350°F. In a large bowl, cream the butter and eggs. Add the Brownie Mix and stir until the mixture is well blended. Spread batter into a lightly greased or sprayed 9 x 12 inch pan. Bake for 30 to 35 minutes. Cool in pan. Cut into 2-inch squares.

Brownies
Makes 24 bars

1 jar Brownie Mix

4 eggs, slightly beaten

3/4 C. butter or margarine,
softened

Preheat the oven to 350°F. In a large bowl, cream the butter and eggs. Add the Brownie Mix and stir until the mixture is well blended. Spread batter into a lightly greased or sprayed 9 x 12 inch pan. Bake for 30 to 35 minutes. Cool in pan. Cut into 2-inch squares.

Brownies
Makes 24 bars

1 jar Brownie Mix

4 eggs, slightly beaten

3/4 C. butter or margarine,
softened

Preheat the oven to 350°F. In a large bowl, cream the butter and eggs. Add the Brownie Mix and stir until the mixture is well blended. Spread batter into a lightly greased or sprayed 9 x 12 inch pan. Bake for 30 to 35 minutes. Cool in pan. Cut into 2-inch squares.

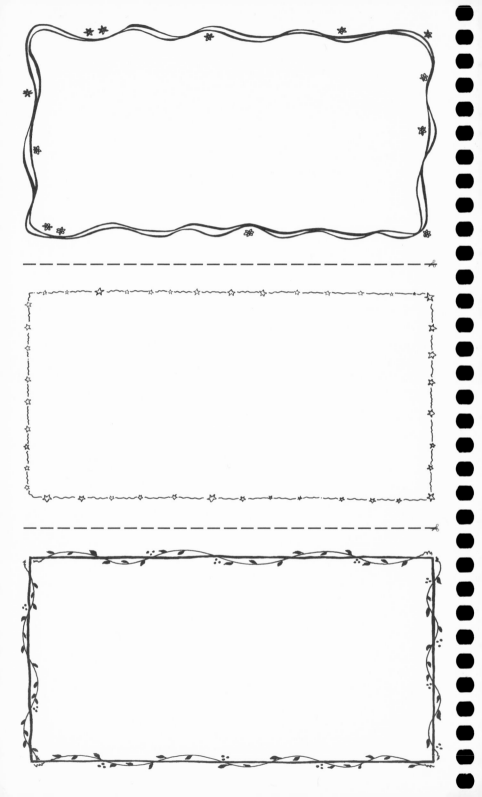

Double Fudge Brownie Mix

1 1/2 C. sugar
3/4 C. cocoa powder (clean
    inside of jar with a paper towel
    after this layer)
3/4 C. all-purpose flour
3/4 C. chocolate chips
1/2 C. chopped pecans, optional

Layer the ingredients in the order given into a wide-mouth 1-quart canning jar. Pack each layer in place before adding the next ingredient.

Attach a gift tag with the mixing and baking directions.

Double Fudge Brownies

Makes 24 bars

1 jar Double Fudge Brownie Mix
3/4 C. butter or margarine,
   softened
3 eggs, slightly beaten

Preheat the oven to 325°F. In a large bowl, cream the butter and eggs. Add the Double Fudge Brownie Mix and stir until the mixture is well blended. Spread batter into a lightly greased or sprayed 9 x 12 inch pan. Bake for 30 to 40 minutes. Cool in pan. Cut into 2-inch squares.

Double Fudge Brownies
Makes 24 bars

1 jar Double Fudge Brownie Mix   3 eggs, slightly beaten
3/4 C. butter or margarine,
   softened

Preheat the oven to 325°F. In a large bowl, cream the butter and eggs. Add the Double Fudge Brownie Mix and stir until the mixture is well blended. Spread batter into a lightly greased or sprayed 9 x 12 inch pan. Bake for 30 to 40 minutes. Cool in pan. Cut into 2-inch squares.

Double Fudge Brownies
Makes 24 bars

1 jar Double Fudge Brownie Mix   3 eggs, slightly beaten
3/4 C. butter or margarine,
   softened

Preheat the oven to 325°F. In a large bowl, cream the butter and eggs. Add the Double Fudge Brownie Mix and stir until the mixture is well blended. Spread batter into a lightly greased or sprayed 9 x 12 inch pan. Bake for 30 to 40 minutes. Cool in pan. Cut into 2-inch squares.

Double Fudge Brownies
Makes 24 bars

1 jar Double Fudge Brownie Mix   3 eggs, slightly beaten
3/4 C. butter or margarine,
   softened

Preheat the oven to 325°F. In a large bowl, cream the butter and eggs. Add the Double Fudge Brownie Mix and stir until the mixture is well blended. Spread batter into a lightly greased or sprayed 9 x 12 inch pan. Bake for 30 to 40 minutes. Cool in pan. Cut into 2-inch squares.

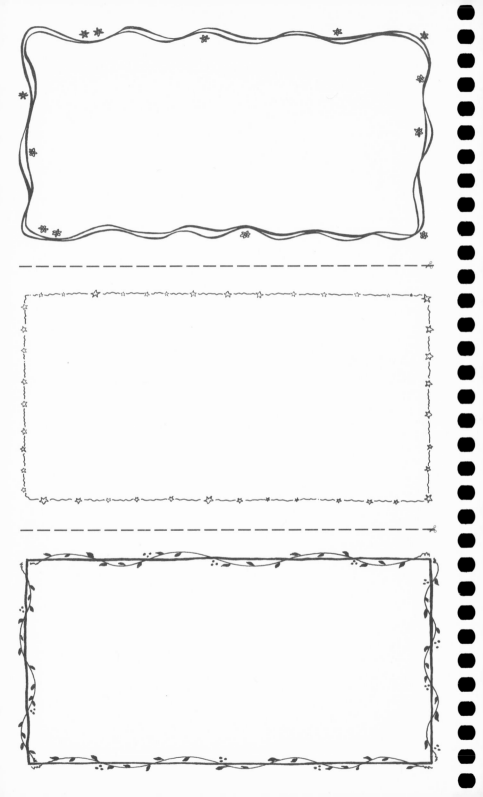

Double Fudge Brownies
Makes 24 bars

1 jar Double Fudge Brownie Mix
3/4 C. butter or margarine,
    softened

3 eggs, slightly beaten

Preheat the oven to 325°F. In a large bowl, cream the butter and eggs. Add the Double Fudge Brownie Mix and stir until the mixture is well blended. Spread batter into a lightly greased or sprayed 9 x 12 inch pan. Bake for 30 to 40 minutes. Cool in pan. Cut into 2-inch squares.

Double Fudge Brownies
Makes 24 bars

1 jar Double Fudge Brownie Mix
3/4 C. butter or margarine,
    softened

3 eggs, slightly beaten

Preheat the oven to 325°F. In a large bowl, cream the butter and eggs. Add the Double Fudge Brownie Mix and stir until the mixture is well blended. Spread batter into a lightly greased or sprayed 9 x 12 inch pan. Bake for 30 to 40 minutes. Cool in pan. Cut into 2-inch squares.

Double Fudge Brownies
Makes 24 bars

1 jar Double Fudge Brownie Mix
3/4 C. butter or margarine,
    softened

3 eggs, slightly beaten

Preheat the oven to 325°F. In a large bowl, cream the butter and eggs. Add the Double Fudge Brownie Mix and stir until the mixture is well blended. Spread batter into a lightly greased or sprayed 9 x 12 inch pan. Bake for 30 to 40 minutes. Cool in pan. Cut into 2-inch squares.

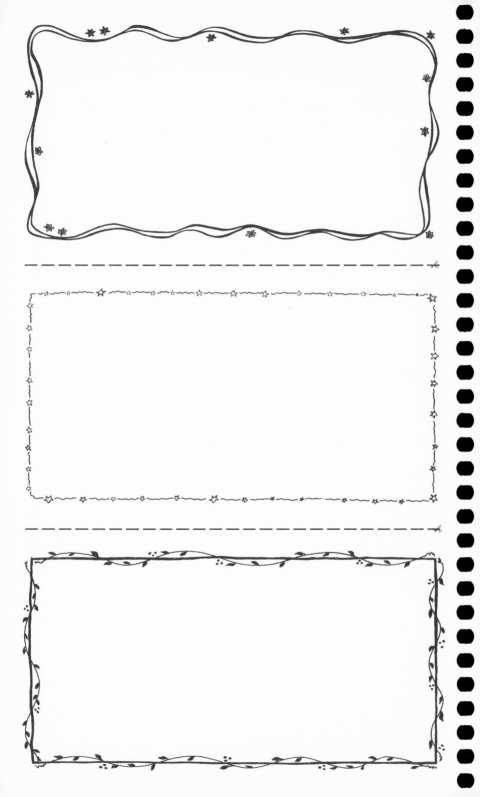

Butterscotch Brownie Mix

1/2 C. flaked coconut
3/4 C. chopped pecans
1 3/4 C. brown sugar
2 C. flour
1 1/2 T. baking powder
1/4 tsp. salt

Layer the ingredients in the order given into a wide-mouth 1-quart canning jar. Pack each layer in place before adding the next ingredient.

Attach a gift tag with the mixing and baking directions.

Butterscotch Brownies

Makes 24 bars

1 jar Butterscotch Brownie Mix
3/4 C. butter or margarine,
  softened
2 eggs, slightly beaten
2 tsp. vanilla

Preheat the oven to 375°F. In a large bowl, cream the butter, eggs and vanilla. Add the Butterscotch Brownie Mix and stir until the mixture is well blended. Spread batter into a lightly greased or sprayed 9 x 12 inch pan. Bake for 25 to 30minutes. Cool in pan. Cut into 2-inch squares.

Butterscotch Brownies
Makes 24 bars

1 jar Butterscotch Brownie Mix
3/4 C. butter or margarine,
   softened

2 eggs, slightly beaten
2 tsp. vanilla

    Preheat the oven to 375°F. In a large bowl, cream the butter, eggs and vanilla. Add the Butterscotch Brownie Mix and stir until the mixture is well blended. Spread batter into a lightly greased or sprayed 9 x 12 inch pan. Bake for 25 to 30 minutes. Cool in pan. Cut into 2-inch squares.

Butterscotch Brownies
Makes 24 bars

1 jar Butterscotch Brownie Mix
3/4 C. butter or margarine,
   softened

2 eggs, slightly beaten
2 tsp. vanilla

    Preheat the oven to 375°F. In a large bowl, cream the butter, eggs and vanilla. Add the Butterscotch Brownie Mix and stir until the mixture is well blended. Spread batter into a lightly greased or sprayed 9 x 12 inch pan. Bake for 25 to 30 minutes. Cool in pan. Cut into 2-inch squares.

Butterscotch Brownies
Makes 24 bars

1 jar Butterscotch Brownie Mix
3/4 C. butter or margarine,
   softened

2 eggs, slightly beaten
2 tsp. vanilla

    Preheat the oven to 375°F. In a large bowl, cream the butter, eggs and vanilla. Add the Butterscotch Brownie Mix and stir until the mixture is well blended. Spread batter into a lightly greased or sprayed 9 x 12 inch pan. Bake for 25 to 30 minutes. Cool in pan. Cut into 2-inch squares.

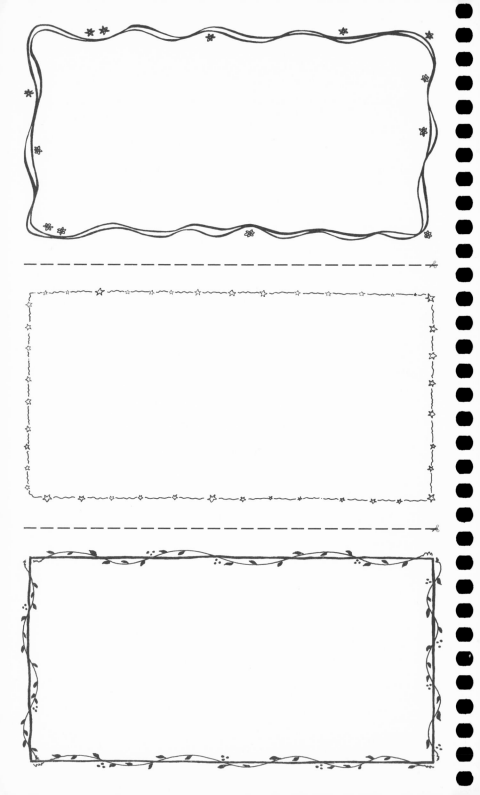

Butterscotch Brownies
Makes 24 bars

1 jar Butterscotch Brownie Mix
3/4 C. butter or margarine,
 softened

2 eggs, slightly beaten
2 tsp. vanilla

Preheat the oven to 375°F. In a large bowl, cream the butter, eggs and vanilla. Add the Butterscotch Brownie Mix and stir until the mixture is well blended. Spread batter into a lightly greased or sprayed 9 x 12 inch pan. Bake for 25 to 30 minutes. Cool in pan. Cut into 2-inch squares.

Butterscotch Brownies
Makes 24 bars

1 jar Butterscotch Brownie Mix
3/4 C. butter or margarine,
 softened

2 eggs, slightly beaten
2 tsp. vanilla

Preheat the oven to 375°F. In a large bowl, cream the butter, eggs and vanilla. Add the Butterscotch Brownie Mix and stir until the mixture is well blended. Spread batter into a lightly greased or sprayed 9 x 12 inch pan. Bake for 25 to 30 minutes. Cool in pan. Cut into 2-inch squares.

Butterscotch Brownies
Makes 24 bars

1 jar Butterscotch Brownie Mix
3/4 C. butter or margarine,
 softened

2 eggs, slightly beaten
2 tsp. vanilla

Preheat the oven to 375°F. In a large bowl, cream the butter, eggs and vanilla. Add the Butterscotch Brownie Mix and stir until the mixture is well blended. Spread batter into a lightly greased or sprayed 9 x 12 inch pan. Bake for 25 to 30 minutes. Cool in pan. Cut into 2-inch squares.

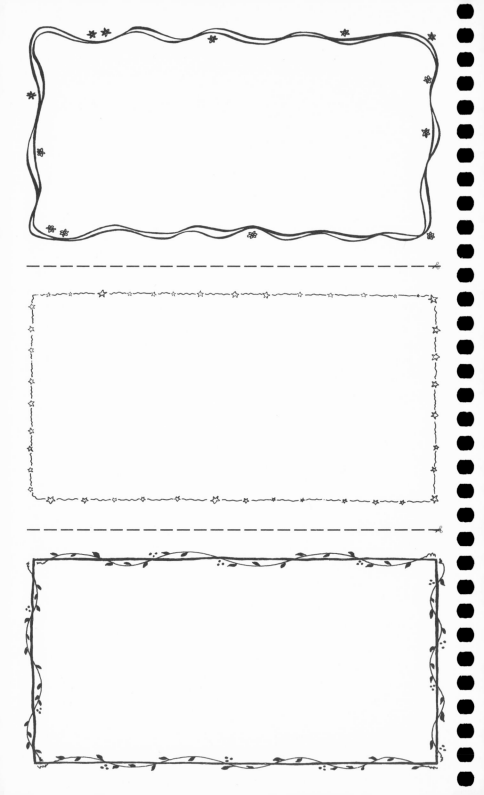

Sand Art
Brownie Mix

1/2 tsp. salt
1 1/2 C. all-purpose flour
1/3 C. cocoa powder (clean
   inside of jar with a paper
   towel after this layer)
1/2 C. all-purpose flour
2/3 C. brown sugar
2/3 C. sugar
1/2 C. chocolate chips
1/2 C. white chocolate chips

   Layer the ingredients in the order given into a wide-mouth 1-quart canning jar. Pack each layer in place before adding the next ingredient.

   Attach a gift tag with the mixing and baking directions.

❀ *A half-yard of fabric should make eight wide-mouth jar covers.* ❀

Sand Art Brownies

Makes 16 bars

1 jar Sand Art Brownie Mix
2/3 C. vegetable oil
3 eggs, slightly beaten
1 tsp. vanilla
Walnuts or pecans, optional

Preheat the oven to 350°F. In a large bowl, mix the oil, eggs and vanilla. Add the Sand Art Brownie Mix and stir until the mixture is well blended. Add nuts if desired. Spread batter into a lightly greased or sprayed 8 x 8 inch pan. Bake for 35 to 40 minutes. Cool in pan. Cut into 2-inch squares.

Sand Art Brownies
Makes 16 bars

1 jar Sand Art Brownie Mix
2/3 C. vegetable oil
3 eggs, slightly beaten

1 tsp. vanilla
Walnuts or pecans, optional

Preheat the oven to 350°F. In a large bowl, mix the oil, eggs and vanilla. Add the Sand Art Brownie Mix and stir until the mixture is well blended. Add nuts if desired. Spread batter into a lightly greased or sprayed 8 x 8 inch pan. Bake for 35 to 40 minutes. Cool in pan. Cut into 2-inch squares.

Sand Art Brownies
Makes 16 bars

1 jar Sand Art Brownie Mix
2/3 C. vegetable oil
3 eggs, slightly beaten

1 tsp. vanilla
Walnuts or pecans, optional

Preheat the oven to 350°F. In a large bowl, mix the oil, eggs and vanilla. Add the Sand Art Brownie Mix and stir until the mixture is well blended. Add nuts if desired. Spread batter into a lightly greased or sprayed 8 x 8 inch pan. Bake for 35 to 40 minutes. Cool in pan. Cut into 2-inch squares.

Sand Art Brownies
Makes 16 bars

1 jar Sand Art Brownie Mix
2/3 C. vegetable oil
3 eggs, slightly beaten

1 tsp. vanilla
Walnuts or pecans, optional

Preheat the oven to 350°F. In a large bowl, mix the oil, eggs and vanilla. Add the Sand Art Brownie Mix and stir until the mixture is well blended. Add nuts if desired. Spread batter into a lightly greased or sprayed 8 x 8 inch pan. Bake for 35 to 40 minutes. Cool in pan. Cut into 2-inch squares.

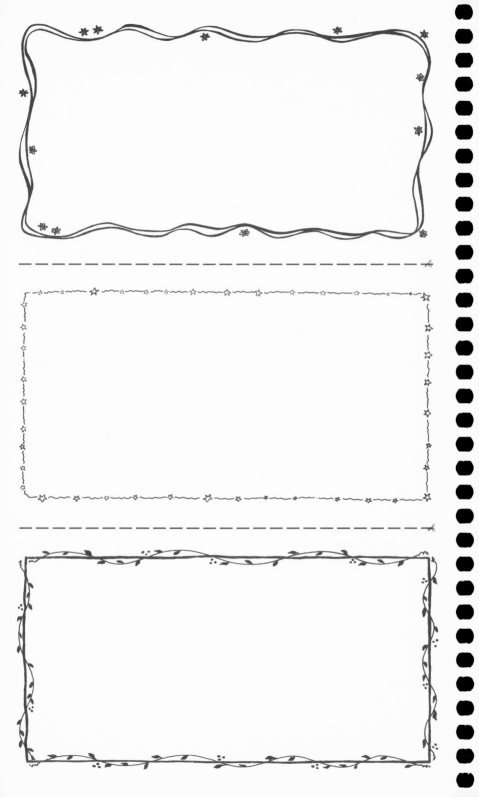

Sand Art Brownies
Makes 16 bars

1 jar Sand Art Brownie Mix
2/3 C. vegetable oil
3 eggs, slightly beaten

1 tsp. vanilla
Walnuts or pecans, optional

Preheat the oven to 350°F. In a large bowl, mix the oil, eggs and vanilla. Add the Sand Art Brownie Mix and stir until the mixture is well blended. Add nuts if desired. Spread batter into a lightly greased or sprayed 8 x 8 inch pan. Bake for 35 to 40 minutes. Cool in pan. Cut into 2-inch squares.

Sand Art Brownies
Makes 16 bars

1 jar Sand Art Brownie Mix
2/3 C. vegetable oil
3 eggs, slightly beaten

1 tsp. vanilla
Walnuts or pecans, optional

Preheat the oven to 350°F. In a large bowl, mix the oil, eggs and vanilla. Add the Sand Art Brownie Mix and stir until the mixture is well blended. Add nuts if desired. Spread batter into a lightly greased or sprayed 8 x 8 inch pan. Bake for 35 to 40 minutes. Cool in pan. Cut into 2-inch squares.

Sand Art Brownies
Makes 16 bars

1 jar Sand Art Brownie Mix
2/3 C. vegetable oil
3 eggs, slightly beaten

1 tsp. vanilla
Walnuts or pecans, optional

Preheat the oven to 350°F. In a large bowl, mix the oil, eggs and vanilla. Add the Sand Art Brownie Mix and stir until the mixture is well blended. Add nuts if desired. Spread batter into a lightly greased or sprayed 8 x 8 inch pan. Bake for 35 to 40 minutes. Cool in pan. Cut into 2-inch squares.

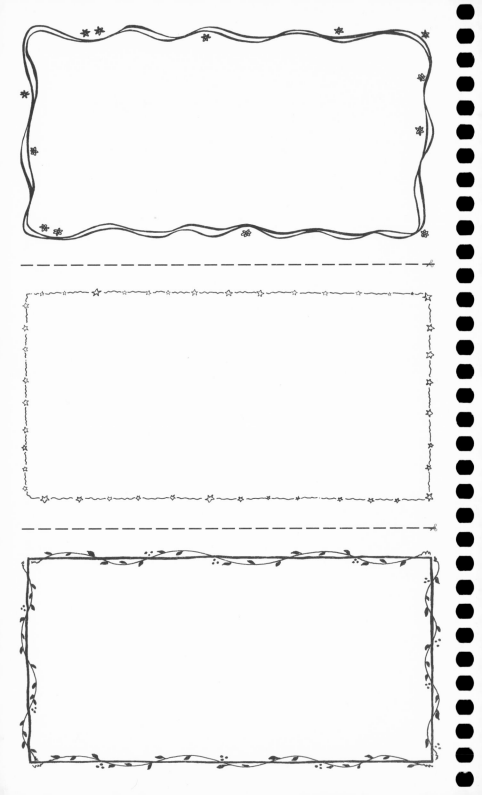

Chewy Butterscotch Nut Bar Mix

1/2 C. butterscotch chips
1/2 C. pieces or coarsely
    chopped pecans, toasted &
    cooled completely
1/2 C. brown sugar
1 C. buttermilk biscuit &
    baking mix
1/2 C. brown sugar
1 C. buttermilk biscuit &
    baking mix

Layer the ingredients in the order given into a wide-mouth 1-quart canning jar. Pack each layer in place before adding the next ingredient.

Attach a gift tag with the mixing and baking directions.

Chewy Butterscotch Nut Bars

Makes 16 bars

1 jar Chewy Butterscotch
   Nut Bar Mix
3/4 C. butter or margarine,
   melted
2 eggs, slightly beaten
1 tsp. vanilla

Preheat the oven to 350°F. In a large bowl, cream the butter, eggs and vanilla. Add the Chewy Butterscotch Nut Bar Mix and stir until the mixture is well blended. Spread batter into a lightly greased or sprayed 8 x 8 inch pan. Bake for 30 to 35 minutes. Cool in pan. Cut into 2-inch squares.

Chewy Butterscotch Nut Bars
Makes 16 bars

1 jar Chewy Butterscotch
  Nut Bar Mix
3/4 C. butter or margarine,
  melted

2 eggs, slightly beaten
1 tsp. vanilla

Preheat the oven to 350°F. In a large bowl, cream the butter, eggs and vanilla. Add the Chewy Butterscotch Nut Bar Mix and stir until the mixture is well blended. Spread batter into a lightly greased or sprayed 8 x 8 inch pan. Bake for 30 to 35 minutes. Cool in pan. Cut into 2-inch squares.

Chewy Butterscotch Nut Bars
Makes 16 bars

1 jar Chewy Butterscotch
  Nut Bar Mix
3/4 C. butter or margarine,
  melted

2 eggs, slightly beaten
1 tsp. vanilla

Preheat the oven to 350°F. In a large bowl, cream the butter, eggs and vanilla. Add the Chewy Butterscotch Nut Bar Mix and stir until the mixture is well blended. Spread batter into a lightly greased or sprayed 8 x 8 inch pan. Bake for 30 to 35 minutes. Cool in pan. Cut into 2-inch squares.

Chewy Butterscotch Nut Bars
Makes 16 bars

1 jar Chewy Butterscotch
  Nut Bar Mix
3/4 C. butter or margarine,
  melted

2 eggs, slightly beaten
1 tsp. vanilla

Preheat the oven to 350°F. In a large bowl, cream the butter, eggs and vanilla. Add the Chewy Butterscotch Nut Bar Mix and stir until the mixture is well blended. Spread batter into a lightly greased or sprayed 8 x 8 inch pan. Bake for 30 to 35 minutes. Cool in pan. Cut into 2-inch squares.

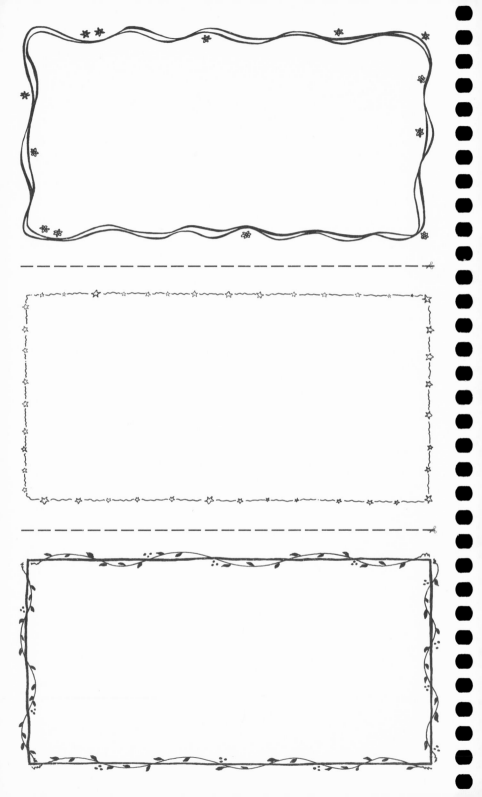

Chewy Butterscotch Nut Bars
Makes 16 bars

1 jar Chewy Butterscotch
 Nut Bar Mix
3/4 C. butter or margarine,
 melted

2 eggs, slightly beaten
1 tsp. vanilla

Preheat the oven to 350°F. In a large bowl, cream the butter, eggs and vanilla. Add the Chewy Butterscotch Nut Bar Mix and stir until the mixture is well blended. Spread batter into a lightly greased or sprayed 8 x 8 inch pan. Bake for 30 to 35 minutes. Cool in pan. Cut into 2-inch squares.

Chewy Butterscotch Nut Bars
Makes 16 bars

1 jar Chewy Butterscotch
 Nut Bar Mix
3/4 C. butter or margarine,
 melted

2 eggs, slightly beaten
1 tsp. vanilla

Preheat the oven to 350°F. In a large bowl, cream the butter, eggs and vanilla. Add the Chewy Butterscotch Nut Bar Mix and stir until the mixture is well blended. Spread batter into a lightly greased or sprayed 8 x 8 inch pan. Bake for 30 to 35 minutes. Cool in pan. Cut into 2-inch squares.

Chewy Butterscotch Nut Bars
Makes 16 bars

1 jar Chewy Butterscotch
 Nut Bar Mix
3/4 C. butter or margarine,
 melted

2 eggs, slightly beaten
1 tsp. vanilla

Preheat the oven to 350°F. In a large bowl, cream the butter, eggs and vanilla. Add the Chewy Butterscotch Nut Bar Mix and stir until the mixture is well blended. Spread batter into a lightly greased or sprayed 8 x 8 inch pan. Bake for 30 to 35 minutes. Cool in pan. Cut into 2-inch squares.

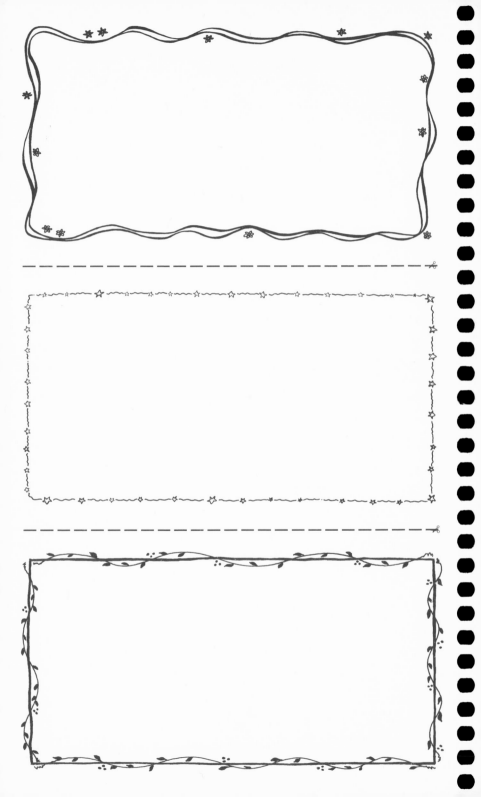

White Christmas Bar Mix

1/2 C. white chocolate chips
1/2 C. sliced almonds, toasted
   & cooled completely
1/2 C. brown sugar
1 C. buttermilk biscuit &
   baking mix
1/2 C. brown sugar
1 C. buttermilk biscuit &
   baking mix

Layer the ingredients in the order given into a wide-mouth 1-quart canning jar. Pack each layer in place before adding the next ingredient.

Attach a gift tag with the mixing and baking directions.

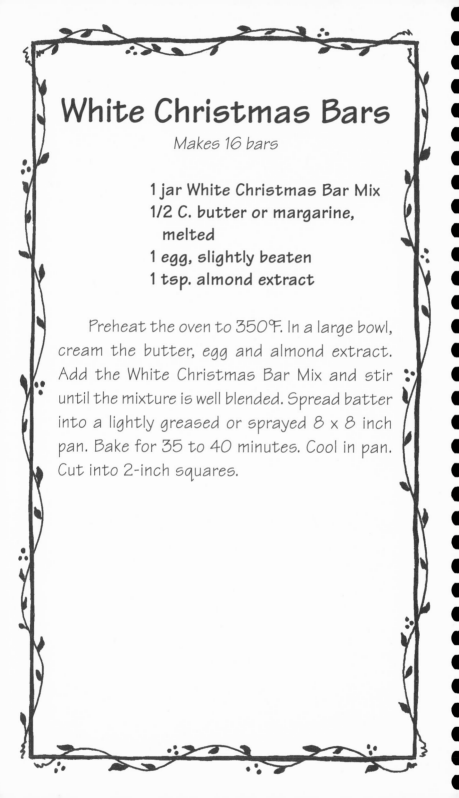

White Christmas Bars

Makes 16 bars

1 jar White Christmas Bar Mix
1/2 C. butter or margarine,
   melted
1 egg, slightly beaten
1 tsp. almond extract

Preheat the oven to 350°F. In a large bowl, cream the butter, egg and almond extract. Add the White Christmas Bar Mix and stir until the mixture is well blended. Spread batter into a lightly greased or sprayed 8 x 8 inch pan. Bake for 35 to 40 minutes. Cool in pan. Cut into 2-inch squares.

White Christmas Bars
Makes 16 bars

1 jar White Christmas Bar Mix
1/2 C. butter or margarine,
  melted

1 egg, slightly beaten
1 tsp. almond extract

Preheat the oven to 350°F. In a large bowl, cream the butter, egg and almond extract. Add the White Christmas Bar Mix and stir until the mixture is well blended. Spread batter into a lightly greased or sprayed 8 x 8 inch pan. Bake for 35 to 40 minutes. Cool in pan. Cut into 2-inch squares.

White Christmas Bars
Makes 16 bars

1 jar White Christmas Bar Mix
1/2 C. butter or margarine,
  melted

1 egg, slightly beaten
1 tsp. almond extract

Preheat the oven to 350°F. In a large bowl, cream the butter, egg and almond extract. Add the White Christmas Bar Mix and stir until the mixture is well blended. Spread batter into a lightly greased or sprayed 8 x 8 inch pan. Bake for 35 to 40 minutes. Cool in pan. Cut into 2-inch squares.

White Christmas Bars
Makes 16 bars

1 jar White Christmas Bar Mix
1/2 C. butter or margarine,
  melted

1 egg, slightly beaten
1 tsp. almond extract

Preheat the oven to 350°F. In a large bowl, cream the butter, egg and almond extract. Add the White Christmas Bar Mix and stir until the mixture is well blended. Spread batter into a lightly greased or sprayed 8 x 8 inch pan. Bake for 35 to 40 minutes. Cool in pan. Cut into 2-inch squares.

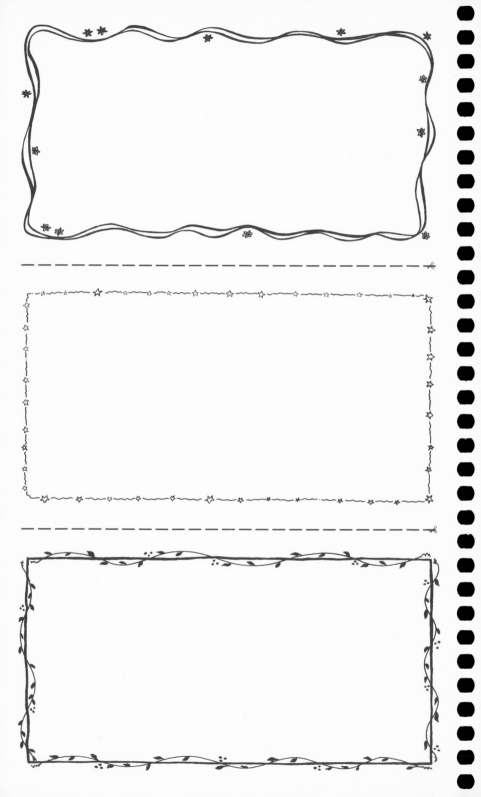

White Christmas Bars
Makes 16 bars

1 jar White Christmas Bar Mix
1/2 C. butter or margarine,
   melted

1 egg, slightly beaten
1 tsp. almond extract

    Preheat the oven to 350°F. In a large bowl, cream the butter, egg and almond extract. Add the White Christmas Bar Mix and stir until the mixture is well blended. Spread batter into a lightly greased or sprayed 8 x 8 inch pan. Bake for 35 to 40 minutes. Cool in pan. Cut into 2-inch squares.

White Christmas Bars
Makes 16 bars

1 jar White Christmas Bar Mix
1/2 C. butter or margarine,
   melted

1 egg, slightly beaten
1 tsp. almond extract

    Preheat the oven to 350°F. In a large bowl, cream the butter, egg and almond extract. Add the White Christmas Bar Mix and stir until the mixture is well blended. Spread batter into a lightly greased or sprayed 8 x 8 inch pan. Bake for 35 to 40 minutes. Cool in pan. Cut into 2-inch squares.

White Christmas Bars
Makes 16 bars

1 jar White Christmas Bar Mix
1/2 C. butter or margarine,
   melted

1 egg, slightly beaten
1 tsp. almond extract

    Preheat the oven to 350°F. In a large bowl, cream the butter, egg and almond extract. Add the White Christmas Bar Mix and stir until the mixture is well blended. Spread batter into a lightly greased or sprayed 8 x 8 inch pan. Bake for 35 to 40 minutes. Cool in pan. Cut into 2-inch squares.

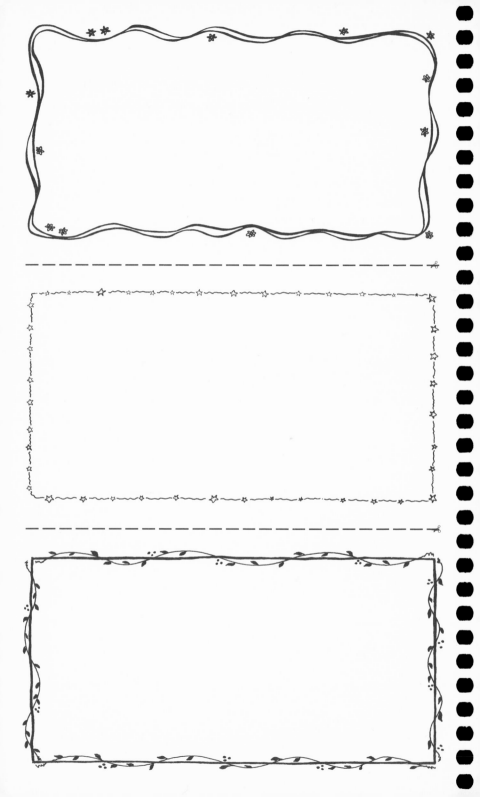

Chocolate Chip Bar Mix

1 tsp. baking powder
1 tsp. baking soda
1/2 tsp. salt
3/4 C. all-purpose flour
1/4 C. sugar
1/4 C. brown sugar
1 C. chocolate chips
1/2 C. brown sugar
1/4 C. sugar
1 C. all-purpose flour

Layer the ingredients in the order given into a wide-mouth 1-quart canning jar. Pack each layer in place before adding the next ingredient.

Attach a gift tag with the mixing and baking directions.

Chocolate Chip Bars

Makes 24 bars

1 jar Chocolate Chip Bar Mix
3/4 C. butter or margarine,
  softened
2 eggs, slightly beaten
1/2 tsp. vanilla

Preheat the oven to 375°F. In a large bowl, cream the butter, eggs and vanilla. Add the Chocolate Chip Bar Mix and stir until the mixture is well blended. Spread batter into a lightly greased or sprayed 9 x 12 inch pan. Bake for 20 to 25 minutes. Cool in pan. Cut into 2-inch squares.

Chocolate Chip Bars
Makes 24 bars

1 jar Chocolate Chip Bar Mix
3/4 C. butter or margarine,
   softened

2 eggs, slightly beaten
1/2 tsp. vanilla

Preheat the oven to 375°F. In a large bowl, cream the butter, eggs and vanilla. Add the Chocolate Chip Bar Mix and stir until the mixture is well blended. Spread batter into a lightly greased or sprayed 9 x 12 inch pan. Bake for 20 to 25 minutes. Cool in pan. Cut into 2-inch squares.

Chocolate Chip Bars
Makes 24 bars

1 jar Chocolate Chip Bar Mix
3/4 C. butter or margarine,
   softened

2 eggs, slightly beaten
1/2 tsp. vanilla

Preheat the oven to 375°F. In a large bowl, cream the butter, eggs and vanilla. Add the Chocolate Chip Bar Mix and stir until the mixture is well blended. Spread batter into a lightly greased or sprayed 9 x 12 inch pan. Bake for 20 to 25 minutes. Cool in pan. Cut into 2-inch squares.

Chocolate Chip Bars
Makes 24 bars

1 jar Chocolate Chip Bar Mix
3/4 C. butter or margarine,
   softened

2 eggs, slightly beaten
1/2 tsp. vanilla

Preheat the oven to 375°F. In a large bowl, cream the butter, eggs and vanilla. Add the Chocolate Chip Bar Mix and stir until the mixture is well blended. Spread batter into a lightly greased or sprayed 9 x 12 inch pan. Bake for 20 to 25 minutes. Cool in pan. Cut into 2-inch squares.

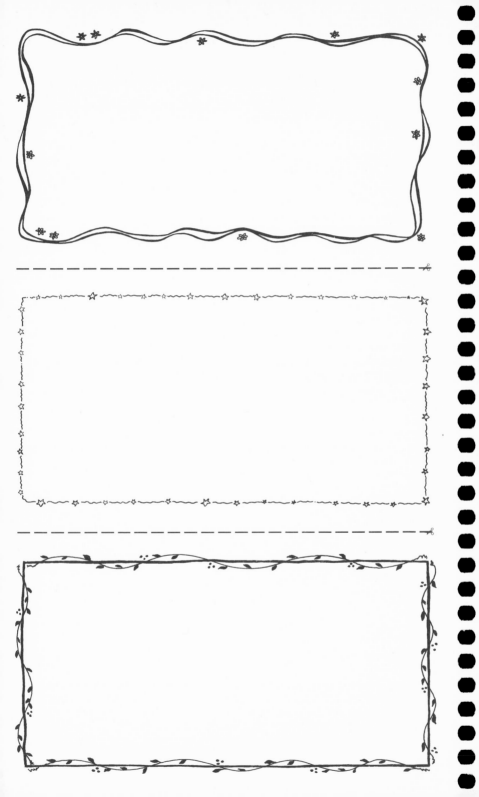

Chocolate Chip Bars
Makes 24 bars

1 jar Chocolate Chip Bar Mix
3/4 C. butter or margarine,
  softened

2 eggs, slightly beaten
1/2 tsp. vanilla

  Preheat the oven to 375°F. In a large bowl, cream the butter, eggs and vanilla. Add the Chocolate Chip Bar Mix and stir until the mixture is well blended. Spread batter into a lightly greased or sprayed 9 x 12 inch pan. Bake for 20 to 25 minutes. Cool in pan. Cut into 2-inch squares.

Chocolate Chip Bars
Makes 24 bars

1 jar Chocolate Chip Bar Mix
3/4 C. butter or margarine,
  softened

2 eggs, slightly beaten
1/2 tsp. vanilla

  Preheat the oven to 375°F. In a large bowl, cream the butter, eggs and vanilla. Add the Chocolate Chip Bar Mix and stir until the mixture is well blended. Spread batter into a lightly greased or sprayed 9 x 12 inch pan. Bake for 20 to 25 minutes. Cool in pan. Cut into 2-inch squares.

Chocolate Chip Bars
Makes 24 bars

1 jar Chocolate Chip Bar Mix
3/4 C. butter or margarine,
  softened

2 eggs, slightly beaten
1/2 tsp. vanilla

  Preheat the oven to 375°F. In a large bowl, cream the butter, eggs and vanilla. Add the Chocolate Chip Bar Mix and stir until the mixture is well blended. Spread batter into a lightly greased or sprayed 9 x 12 inch pan. Bake for 20 to 25 minutes. Cool in pan. Cut into 2-inch squares.

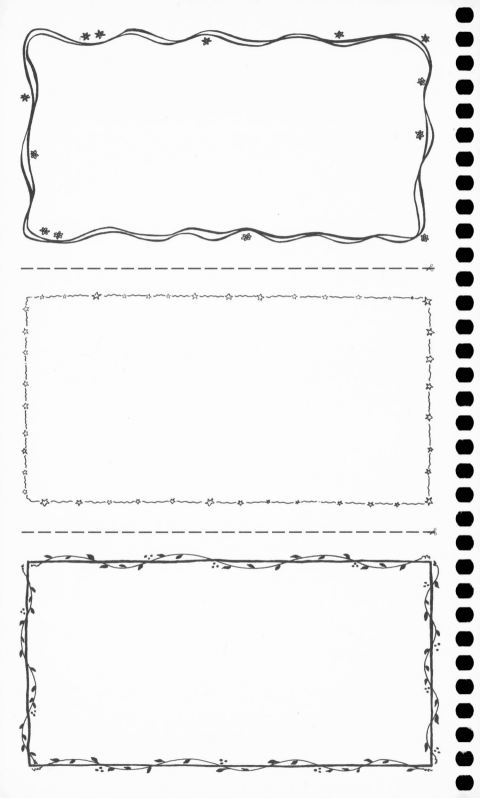

Oatmeal Scotchie Bar Mix

3/4 C. brown sugar
1/2 C. sugar
1/2 C. butterscotch baking
 chips
2 C. old-fashioned oats
1 C. all-purpose flour
1 tsp. ground cinnamon
1 tsp. baking soda
1/2 tsp. salt

Layer the ingredients in the order given into a wide-mouth 1-quart canning jar. Pack each layer in place before adding the next ingredient.

Attach a gift tag with the mixing and baking directions.

Oatmeal Scotchie Bars

Makes 24 bars

1 jar Oatmeal Scotchie Bar Mix
3/4 C. butter or margarine,
  softened
2 eggs, slightly beaten
1 tsp. vanilla

Preheat the oven to 350°F. In a large bowl, cream the butter, eggs and vanilla. Add the Oatmeal Scotchie Bar Mix and stir until the mixture is well blended. Spread batter into a lightly greased or sprayed 9 x 12 inch pan. Bake for 20 to 25 minutes. Cool in pan. Cut into 2-inch squares.

Oatmeal Scotchie Bars
Makes 24 bars

1 jar Oatmeal Scotchie Bar Mix
3/4 C. butter or margarine,
   softened

2 eggs, slightly beaten
1 tsp. vanilla

Preheat the oven to 350°F. In a large bowl, cream the butter, eggs and vanilla. Add the Oatmeal Scotchie Bar Mix and stir until the mixture is well blended. Spread batter into a lightly greased or sprayed 9 x 12 inch pan. Bake for 20 to 25 minutes. Cool in pan. Cut into 2-inch squares.

Oatmeal Scotchie Bars
Makes 24 bars

1 jar Oatmeal Scotchie Bar Mix
3/4 C. butter or margarine,
   softened

2 eggs, slightly beaten
1 tsp. vanilla

Preheat the oven to 350°F. In a large bowl, cream the butter, eggs and vanilla. Add the Oatmeal Scotchie Bar Mix and stir until the mixture is well blended. Spread batter into a lightly greased or sprayed 9 x 12 inch pan. Bake for 20 to 25 minutes. Cool in pan. Cut into 2-inch squares.

Oatmeal Scotchie Bars
Makes 24 bars

1 jar Oatmeal Scotchie Bar Mix
3/4 C. butter or margarine,
   softened

2 eggs, slightly beaten
1 tsp. vanilla

Preheat the oven to 350°F. In a large bowl, cream the butter, eggs and vanilla. Add the Oatmeal Scotchie Bar Mix and stir until the mixture is well blended. Spread batter into a lightly greased or sprayed 9 x 12 inch pan. Bake for 20 to 25 minutes. Cool in pan. Cut into 2-inch squares.

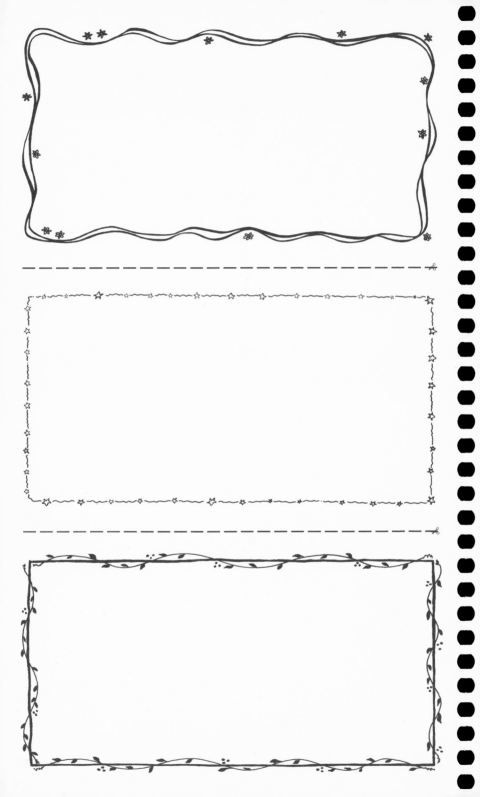

Oatmeal Scotchie Bars
Makes 24 bars

1 jar Oatmeal Scotchie Bar Mix
3/4 C. butter or margarine,
   softened

2 eggs, slightly beaten
1 tsp. vanilla

Preheat the oven to 350°F. In a large bowl, cream the butter, eggs and vanilla. Add the Oatmeal Scotchie Bar Mix and stir until the mixture is well blended. Spread batter into a lightly greased or sprayed 9 x 12 inch pan. Bake for 20 to 25 minutes. Cool in pan. Cut into 2-inch squares.

Oatmeal Scotchie Bars
Makes 24 bars

1 jar Oatmeal Scotchie Bar Mix
3/4 C. butter or margarine,
   softened

2 eggs, slightly beaten
1 tsp. vanilla

Preheat the oven to 350°F. In a large bowl, cream the butter, eggs and vanilla. Add the Oatmeal Scotchie Bar Mix and stir until the mixture is well blended. Spread batter into a lightly greased or sprayed 9 x 12 inch pan. Bake for 20 to 25 minutes. Cool in pan. Cut into 2-inch squares.

Oatmeal Scotchie Bars
Makes 24 bars

1 jar Oatmeal Scotchie Bar Mix
3/4 C. butter or margarine,
   softened

2 eggs, slightly beaten
1 tsp. vanilla

Preheat the oven to 350°F. In a large bowl, cream the butter, eggs and vanilla. Add the Oatmeal Scotchie Bar Mix and stir until the mixture is well blended. Spread batter into a lightly greased or sprayed 9 x 12 inch pan. Bake for 20 to 25 minutes. Cool in pan. Cut into 2-inch squares.

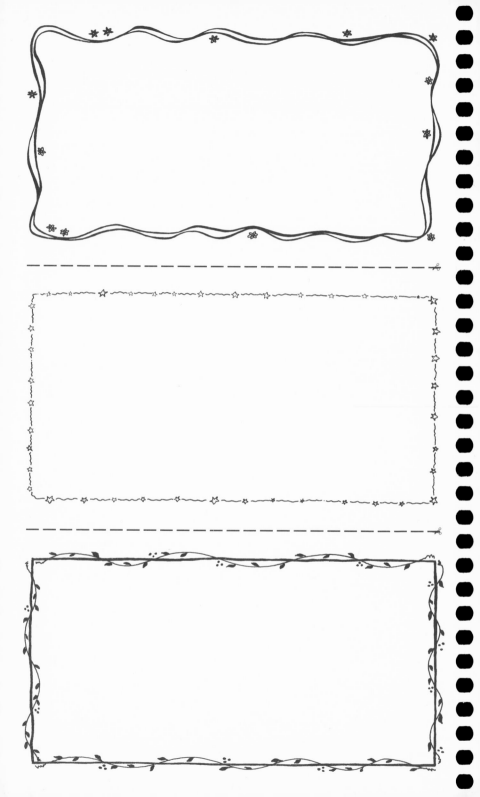

M&M Bar Mix

1 C. M&M candies
2 C. all-purpose flour
1/2 tsp. baking soda
1/2 tsp. baking powder
1 1/4 C. sugar

Layer the ingredients in the order given into a wide-mouth 1-quart canning jar. Pack each layer in place before adding the next ingredient.

Attach a gift tag with the mixing and baking directions.

❀ *These gifts should keep for up to six months. If the mix contains nuts, it should be used within three months.* ❀

M&M Bars

Makes 24 bars

1 jar M&M Bar Mix
3/4 C. butter or margarine,
   softened
2 eggs, slightly beaten
1 tsp. vanilla

Preheat the oven to 375°F. In a large bowl, cream the butter, eggs and vanilla. Add the M&M Bar Mix and stir until the mixture is well blended. Spread batter into a lightly greased or sprayed 9 x 12 inch pan. Bake for 25 to 30 minutes. Cool in pan. Cut into 2-inch squares.

M&M Bars
Makes 24 bars

1 jar M&M Bar Mix
3/4 C. butter or margarine,
  softened

2 eggs, slightly beaten
1 tsp. vanilla

Preheat the oven to 375°F. In a large bowl, cream the butter, eggs and vanilla. Add the M&M Bar Mix and stir until the mixture is well blended. Spread batter into a lightly greased or sprayed 9 x 12 inch pan. Bake for 25 to 30 minutes. Cool in pan. Cut into 2-inch squares.

M&M Bars
Makes 24 bars

1 jar M&M Bar Mix
3/4 C. butter or margarine,
  softened

2 eggs, slightly beaten
1 tsp. vanilla

Preheat the oven to 375°F. In a large bowl, cream the butter, eggs and vanilla. Add the M&M Bar Mix and stir until the mixture is well blended. Spread batter into a lightly greased or sprayed 9 x 12 inch pan. Bake for 25 to 30 minutes. Cool in pan. Cut into 2-inch squares.

M&M Bars
Makes 24 bars

1 jar M&M Bar Mix
3/4 C. butter or margarine,
  softened

2 eggs, slightly beaten
1 tsp. vanilla

Preheat the oven to 375°F. In a large bowl, cream the butter, eggs and vanilla. Add the M&M Bar Mix and stir until the mixture is well blended. Spread batter into a lightly greased or sprayed 9 x 12 inch pan. Bake for 25 to 30 minutes. Cool in pan. Cut into 2-inch squares.

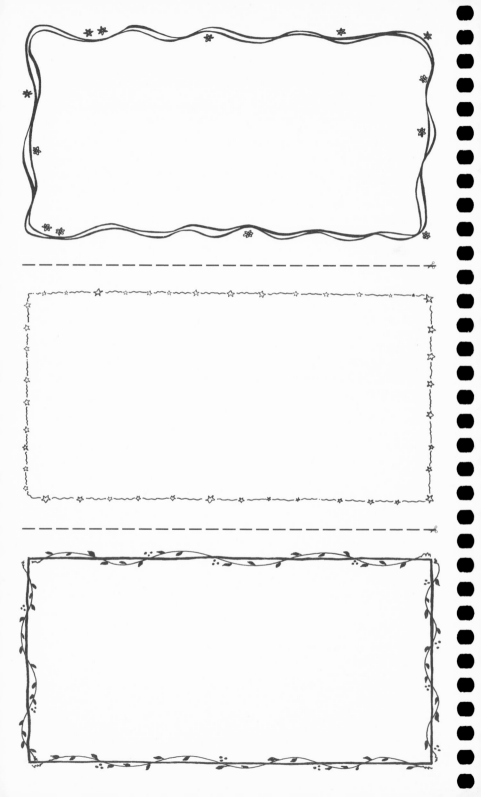

M&M Bars
Makes 24 bars

1 jar M&M Bar Mix
3/4 C. butter or margarine,
  softened

2 eggs, slightly beaten
1 tsp. vanilla

    Preheat the oven to 375°F. In a large bowl, cream the butter, eggs and vanilla. Add the M&M Bar Mix and stir until the mixture is well blended. Spread batter into a lightly greased or sprayed 9 x 12 inch pan. Bake for 25 to 30 minutes. Cool in pan. Cut into 2-inch squares.

M&M Bars
Makes 24 bars

1 jar M&M Bar Mix
3/4 C. butter or margarine,
  softened

2 eggs, slightly beaten
1 tsp. vanilla

    Preheat the oven to 375°F. In a large bowl, cream the butter, eggs and vanilla. Add the M&M Bar Mix and stir until the mixture is well blended. Spread batter into a lightly greased or sprayed 9 x 12 inch pan. Bake for 25 to 30 minutes. Cool in pan. Cut into 2-inch squares.

M&M Bars
Makes 24 bars

1 jar M&M Bar Mix
3/4 C. butter or margarine,
  softened

2 eggs, slightly beaten
1 tsp. vanilla

    Preheat the oven to 375°F. In a large bowl, cream the butter, eggs and vanilla. Add the M&M Bar Mix and stir until the mixture is well blended. Spread batter into a lightly greased or sprayed 9 x 12 inch pan. Bake for 25 to 30 minutes. Cool in pan. Cut into 2-inch squares.

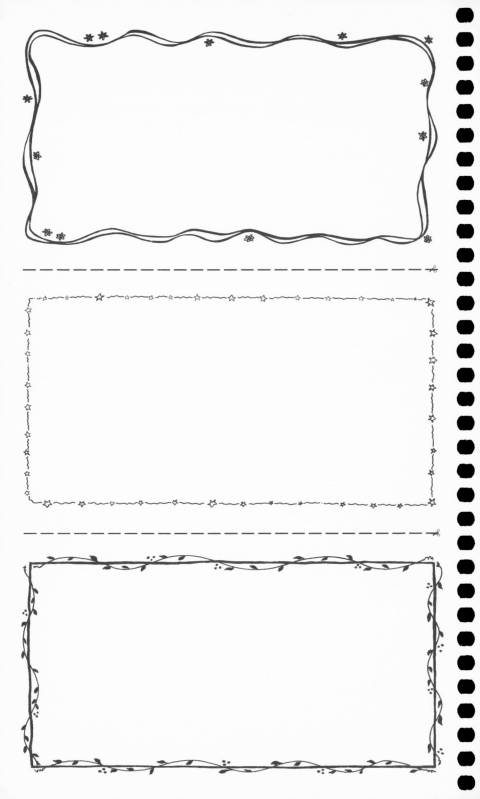

Oatmeal Chocolate Chip Bar Mix

1 C. all-purpose flour
1/2 tsp. baking powder
1/2 tsp. baking soda
1 1/4 C. old-fashioned oats
1/2 C. sugar
1/2 C. brown sugar
1/2 C. chopped nuts
1/2 C. chocolate chips

Layer the ingredients in the order given into a wide-mouth 1-quart canning jar. Pack each layer in place before adding the next ingredient.

Attach a gift tag with the mixing and baking directions.

Oatmeal Chocolate Chip Bars

Makes 24 bars

1 jar Oatmeal Chocolate
   Chip Bar Mix
3/4 C. butter or margarine,
   softened
4 eggs, slightly beaten

Preheat the oven to 375°F. In a large bowl, cream the butter and eggs. Add the Oatmeal Chocolate Chip Bar Mix and stir until the mixture is well blended. Spread batter into a lightly greased or sprayed 9 x 12 inch pan. Bake for 20 to 25 minutes. Cool in pan. Cut into 2-inch squares.

Oatmeal Chocolate Chip Bars
Makes 24 bars

1 jar Oatmeal Chocolate
  Chip Bar Mix
3/4 C. butter or margarine,
  softened

4 eggs, slightly beaten

Preheat the oven to 375°F. In a large bowl, cream the butter and eggs. Add the Oatmeal Chocolate Chip Bar Mix and stir until the mixture is well blended. Spread batter into a lightly greased or sprayed 9 x 12 inch pan. Bake for 20 to 25 minutes. Cool in pan. Cut into 2-inch squares.

Oatmeal Chocolate Chip Bars
Makes 24 bars

1 jar Oatmeal Chocolate
  Chip Bar Mix
3/4 C. butter or margarine,
  softened

4 eggs, slightly beaten

Preheat the oven to 375°F. In a large bowl, cream the butter and eggs. Add the Oatmeal Chocolate Chip Bar Mix and stir until the mixture is well blended. Spread batter into a lightly greased or sprayed 9 x 12 inch pan. Bake for 20 to 25 minutes. Cool in pan. Cut into 2-inch squares.

Oatmeal Chocolate Chip Bars
Makes 24 bars

1 jar Oatmeal Chocolate
  Chip Bar Mix
3/4 C. butter or margarine,
  softened

4 eggs, slightly beaten

Preheat the oven to 375°F. In a large bowl, cream the butter and eggs. Add the Oatmeal Chocolate Chip Bar Mix and stir until the mixture is well blended. Spread batter into a lightly greased or sprayed 9 x 12 inch pan. Bake for 20 to 25 minutes. Cool in pan. Cut into 2-inch squares.

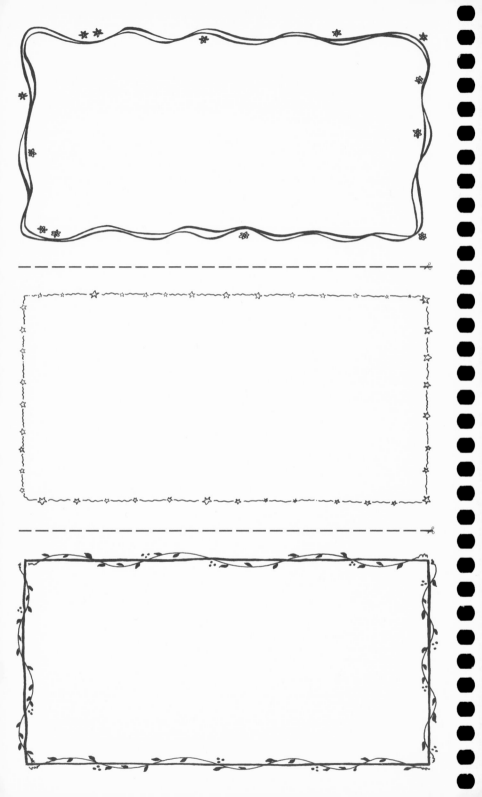

Oatmeal Chocolate Chip Bars
Makes 24 bars

1 jar Oatmeal Chocolate
  Chip Bar Mix
3/4 C. butter or margarine,
  softened

4 eggs, slightly beaten

Preheat the oven to 375°F. In a large bowl, cream the butter and eggs. Add the Oatmeal Chocolate Chip Bar Mix and stir until the mixture is well blended. Spread batter into a lightly greased or sprayed 9 x 12 inch pan. Bake for 20 to 25 minutes. Cool in pan. Cut into 2-inch squares.

Oatmeal Chocolate Chip Bars
Makes 24 bars

1 jar Oatmeal Chocolate
  Chip Bar Mix
3/4 C. butter or margarine,
  softened

4 eggs, slightly beaten

Preheat the oven to 375°F. In a large bowl, cream the butter and eggs. Add the Oatmeal Chocolate Chip Bar Mix and stir until the mixture is well blended. Spread batter into a lightly greased or sprayed 9 x 12 inch pan. Bake for 20 to 25 minutes. Cool in pan. Cut into 2-inch squares.

Oatmeal Chocolate Chip Bars
Makes 24 bars

1 jar Oatmeal Chocolate
  Chip Bar Mix
3/4 C. butter or margarine,
  softened

4 eggs, slightly beaten

Preheat the oven to 375°F. In a large bowl, cream the butter and eggs. Add the Oatmeal Chocolate Chip Bar Mix and stir until the mixture is well blended. Spread batter into a lightly greased or sprayed 9 x 12 inch pan. Bake for 20 to 25 minutes. Cool in pan. Cut into 2-inch squares.

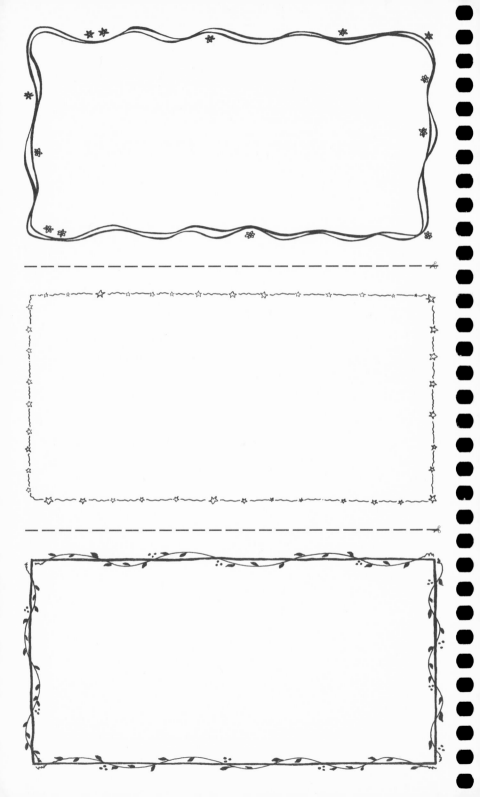

Reese's Peanut Butter Cup Bar Mix

3/4 C. sugar
1/4 C. brown sugar
1 3/4 C. flour
1 tsp. baking powder
1/2 tsp. baking soda
8 large Reese's peanut
    butter cups, cut into 1/2"
    pieces and wrapped in
    plastic wrap

Layer the ingredients in the order given into a wide-mouth 1-quart canning jar. Pack each layer in place before adding the next ingredient.

Attach a gift tag with the mixing and baking directions.

Reese's Peanut Butter Cup Bars

Makes 24 bars

1 jar Reese's Peanut Butter
   Cup Bar Mix
3/4 C. butter or margarine,
   softened
2 eggs, slightly beaten
1 tsp. vanilla

Preheat the oven to 375°F. In a large bowl, cream the butter, eggs and vanilla. Take out Reese's wrapped in plastic and set aside. Add the remaining Reese's Peanut Butter Cup Bar Mix and stir until the mixture is well blended. Stir in Reese's. Spread batter into a lightly greased or sprayed 9 x 12 inch pan. Bake for 13 to 18 minutes. Cool in pan. Cut into 2-inch squares.

Reese's Peanut Butter Cup Bars

Makes 24 bars

1 jar Reese's Peanut Butter
  Cup Bar Mix
3/4 C. butter or margarine,
  softened

2 eggs, slightly beaten
1 tsp. vanilla

Preheat the oven to 375°F. In a large bowl, cream the butter, eggs and vanilla. Take out Reese's wrapped in plastic and set aside. Add the remaining Reese's Peanut Butter Cup Bar Mix and stir until the mixture is well blended. Stir in Reese's. Spread batter into a lightly greased or sprayed 9 x 12 inch pan. Bake for 13 to 18 minutes. Cool in pan. Cut into 2-inch squares.

Reese's Peanut Butter Cup Bars

Makes 24 bars

1 jar Reese's Peanut Butter
  Cup Bar Mix
3/4 C. butter or margarine,
  softened

2 eggs, slightly beaten
1 tsp. vanilla

Preheat the oven to 375°F. In a large bowl, cream the butter, eggs and vanilla. Take out Reese's wrapped in plastic and set aside. Add the remaining Reese's Peanut Butter Cup Bar Mix and stir until the mixture is well blended. Stir in Reese's. Spread batter into a lightly greased or sprayed 9 x 12 inch pan. Bake for 13 to 18 minutes. Cool in pan. Cut into 2-inch squares.

Reese's Peanut Butter Cup Bars

Makes 24 bars

1 jar Reese's Peanut Butter
  Cup Bar Mix
3/4 C. butter or margarine,
  softened

2 eggs, slightly beaten
1 tsp. vanilla

Preheat the oven to 375°F. In a large bowl, cream the butter, eggs and vanilla. Take out Reese's wrapped in plastic and set aside. Add the remaining Reese's Peanut Butter Cup Bar Mix and stir until the mixture is well blended. Stir in Reese's. Spread batter into a lightly greased or sprayed 9 x 12 inch pan. Bake for 13 to 18 minutes. Cool in pan. Cut into 2-inch squares.

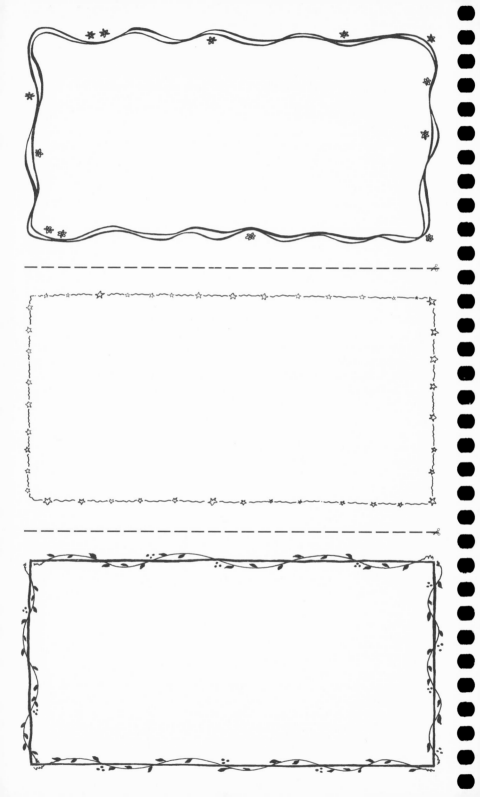

Reese's Peanut Butter Cup Bars
Makes 24 bars

1 jar Reese's Peanut Butter
Cup Bar Mix
3/4 C. butter or margarine,
softened

2 eggs, slightly beaten
1 tsp. vanilla

Preheat the oven to 375°F. In a large bowl, cream the butter, eggs and vanilla. Take out Reese's wrapped in plastic and set aside. Add the remaining Reese's Peanut Butter Cup Bar Mix and stir until the mixture is well blended. Stir in Reese's. Spread batter into a lightly greased or sprayed 9 x 12 inch pan. Bake for 13 to 18 minutes. Cool in pan. Cut into 2-inch squares.

Reese's Peanut Butter Cup Bars
Makes 24 bars

1 jar Reese's Peanut Butter
Cup Bar Mix
3/4 C. butter or margarine,
softened

2 eggs, slightly beaten
1 tsp. vanilla

Preheat the oven to 375°F. In a large bowl, cream the butter, eggs and vanilla. Take out Reese's wrapped in plastic and set aside. Add the remaining Reese's Peanut Butter Cup Bar Mix and stir until the mixture is well blended. Stir in Reese's. Spread batter into a lightly greased or sprayed 9 x 12 inch pan. Bake for 13 to 18 minutes. Cool in pan. Cut into 2-inch squares.

Reese's Peanut Butter Cup Bars
Makes 24 bars

1 jar Reese's Peanut Butter
Cup Bar Mix
3/4 C. butter or margarine,
softened

2 eggs, slightly beaten
1 tsp. vanilla

Preheat the oven to 375°F. In a large bowl, cream the butter, eggs and vanilla. Take out Reese's wrapped in plastic and set aside. Add the remaining Reese's Peanut Butter Cup Bar Mix and stir until the mixture is well blended. Stir in Reese's. Spread batter into a lightly greased or sprayed 9 x 12 inch pan. Bake for 13 to 18 minutes. Cool in pan. Cut into 2-inch squares.

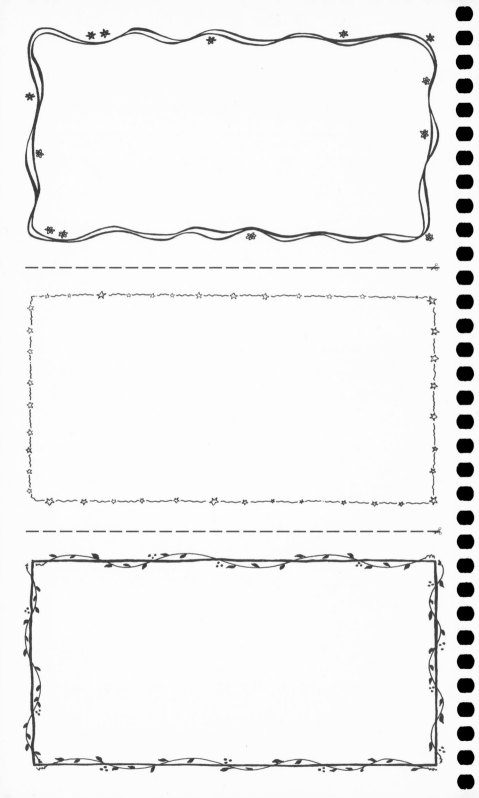

Dreamsicle Bar Mix

1/2 C. Tang instant breakfast
  drink powder
3/4 C. sugar
1 1/4 C. vanilla chips
1 3/4 C. all-purpose flour
1/2 tsp. baking soda
1/2 tsp. baking powder

Layer the ingredients in the order given into a wide-mouth 1-quart canning jar. Pack each layer in place before adding the next ingredient.

Attach a gift tag with the mixing and baking directions.

❋ For an out of the ordinary gift, try placing the mix in a mixing bowl along with kitchen utensils, cookbooks, recipe cards, towels, and pot holders. ❋

Dreamsicle Bars

Makes 24 bars

1 jar Dreamsicle Bar Mix
3/4 C. butter or margarine,
  softened
2 eggs, slightly beaten
1 tsp. vanilla
1 T. water

Preheat the oven to 350°F. In a large bowl, cream the butter, eggs, vanilla and water. Add the Dreamsicle Bar Mix and stir until the mixture is well blended. Spread batter into a lightly greased or sprayed 9 x 12 inch pan. Bake for 20 to 25 minutes. Cool in pan. Cut into 2-inch squares.

Dreamsicle Bars
Makes 24 bars

1 jar Dreamsicle Bar Mix
3/4 C. butter or margarine,
 softened

2 eggs, slightly beaten
1 tsp. vanilla
1 T. water

    Preheat the oven to 350°F. In a large bowl, cream the butter, eggs, vanilla and water. Add the Dreamsicle Bar Mix and stir until the mixture is well blended. Spread batter into a lightly greased or sprayed 9 x 12 inch pan. Bake for 20 to 25 minutes. Cool in pan. Cut into 2-inch squares.

Dreamsicle Bars
Makes 24 bars

1 jar Dreamsicle Bar Mix
3/4 C. butter or margarine,
 softened

2 eggs, slightly beaten
1 tsp. vanilla
1 T. water

    Preheat the oven to 350°F. In a large bowl, cream the butter, eggs, vanilla and water. Add the Dreamsicle Bar Mix and stir until the mixture is well blended. Spread batter into a lightly greased or sprayed 9 x 12 inch pan. Bake for 20 to 25 minutes. Cool in pan. Cut into 2-inch squares.

Dreamsicle Bars
Makes 24 bars

1 jar Dreamsicle Bar Mix
3/4 C. butter or margarine,
 softened

2 eggs, slightly beaten
1 tsp. vanilla
1 T. water

    Preheat the oven to 350°F. In a large bowl, cream the butter, eggs, vanilla and water. Add the Dreamsicle Bar Mix and stir until the mixture is well blended. Spread batter into a lightly greased or sprayed 9 x 12 inch pan. Bake for 20 to 25 minutes. Cool in pan. Cut into 2-inch squares.

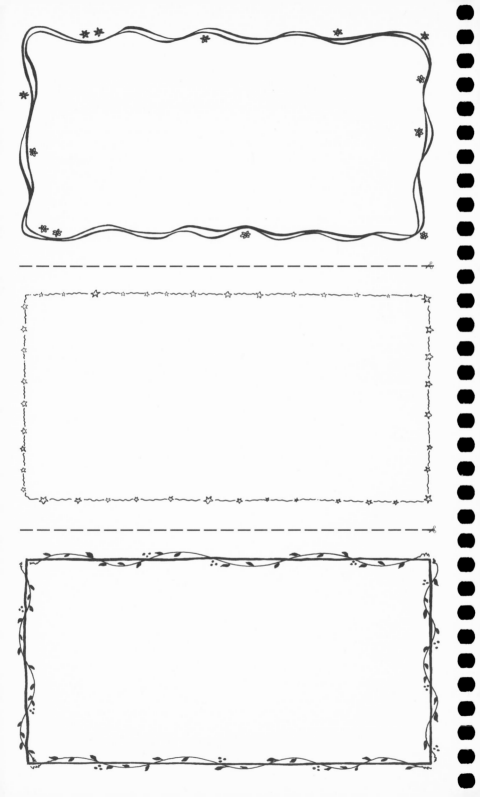

Dreamsicle Bars
Makes 24 bars

1 jar Dreamsicle Bar Mix
3/4 C. butter or margarine,
  softened

2 eggs, slightly beaten
1 tsp. vanilla
1 T. water

    Preheat the oven to 350°F. In a large bowl, cream the butter, eggs, vanilla and water. Add the Dreamsicle Bar Mix and stir until the mixture is well blended. Spread batter into a lightly greased or sprayed 9 x 12 inch pan. Bake for 20 to 25 minutes. Cool in pan. Cut into 2-inch squares.

Dreamsicle Bars
Makes 24 bars

1 jar Dreamsicle Bar Mix
3/4 C. butter or margarine,
  softened

2 eggs, slightly beaten
1 tsp. vanilla
1 T. water

    Preheat the oven to 350°F. In a large bowl, cream the butter, eggs, vanilla and water. Add the Dreamsicle Bar Mix and stir until the mixture is well blended. Spread batter into a lightly greased or sprayed 9 x 12 inch pan. Bake for 20 to 25 minutes. Cool in pan. Cut into 2-inch squares.

Dreamsicle Bars
Makes 24 bars

1 jar Dreamsicle Bar Mix
3/4 C. butter or margarine,
  softened

2 eggs, slightly beaten
1 tsp. vanilla
1 T. water

    Preheat the oven to 350°F. In a large bowl, cream the butter, eggs, vanilla and water. Add the Dreamsicle Bar Mix and stir until the mixture is well blended. Spread batter into a lightly greased or sprayed 9 x 12 inch pan. Bake for 20 to 25 minutes. Cool in pan. Cut into 2-inch squares.

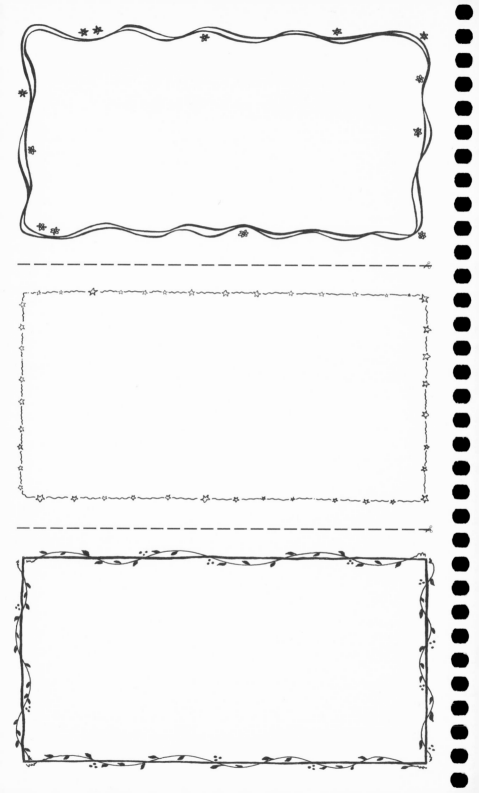

Oatmeal Raisin Bar Mix

3/4 C. brown sugar
1/2 C. sugar
3/4 C. raisins
2 C. old-fashioned oats
1 C. all-purpose flour
3/4 tsp. ground nutmeg
3/4 tsp. baking soda
1/2 tsp. salt

Layer the ingredients in the order given into a wide-mouth 1-quart canning jar. Pack each layer in place before adding the next ingredient.

Attach a gift tag with the mixing and baking directions.

❀ At times, it may seem impossible to make all of the jar ingredients fit, but with persistence, they do all fit. ❀

Oatmeal Raisin Bars

Makes 24 bars

1 jar Oatmeal Raisin Bar Mix
3/4 C. butter or margarine,
  softened
1 egg, slightly beaten
1 tsp. vanilla

Preheat the oven to 350°F. In a large bowl, cream the butter, egg and vanilla. Add the Oatmeal Raisin Bar Mix and stir until the mixture is well blended. Spread batter into a lightly greased or sprayed 9 x 12 inch pan. Bake for 25 to 30 minutes. Cool in pan. Cut into 2-inch squares.

Oatmeal Raisin Bars
Makes 24 bars

1 jar Oatmeal Raisin Bar Mix
3/4 C. butter or margarine,
   softened

1 egg, slightly beaten
1 tsp. vanilla

   Preheat the oven to 350°F. In a large bowl, cream the butter, egg and vanilla. Add the Oatmeal Raisin Bar Mix and stir until the mixture is well blended. Spread batter into a lightly greased or sprayed 9 x 12 inch pan. Bake for 25 to 30 minutes. Cool in pan. Cut into 2-inch squares.

Oatmeal Raisin Bars
Makes 24 bars

1 jar Oatmeal Raisin Bar Mix
3/4 C. butter or margarine,
   softened

1 egg, slightly beaten
1 tsp. vanilla

   Preheat the oven to 350°F. In a large bowl, cream the butter, egg and vanilla. Add the Oatmeal Raisin Bar Mix and stir until the mixture is well blended. Spread batter into a lightly greased or sprayed 9 x 12 inch pan. Bake for 25 to 30 minutes. Cool in pan. Cut into 2-inch squares.

Oatmeal Raisin Bars
Makes 24 bars

1 jar Oatmeal Raisin Bar Mix
3/4 C. butter or margarine,
   softened

1 egg, slightly beaten
1 tsp. vanilla

   Preheat the oven to 350°F. In a large bowl, cream the butter, egg and vanilla. Add the Oatmeal Raisin Bar Mix and stir until the mixture is well blended. Spread batter into a lightly greased or sprayed 9 x 12 inch pan. Bake for 25 to 30 minutes. Cool in pan. Cut into 2-inch squares.

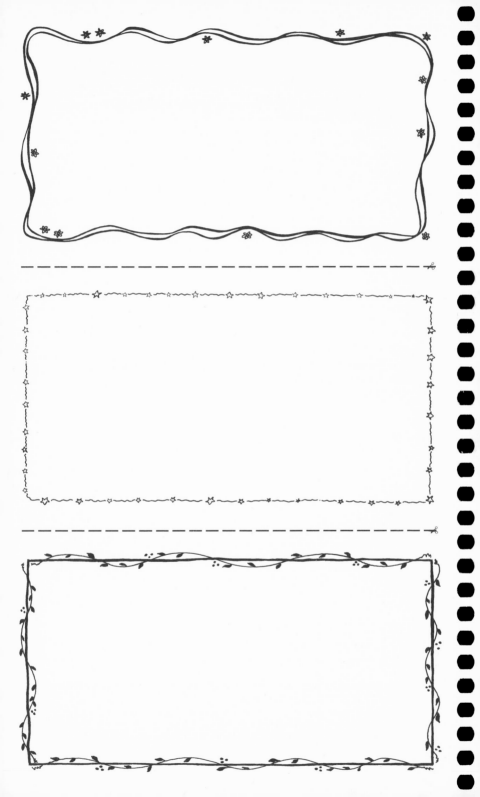

Oatmeal Raisin Bars
Makes 24 bars

1 jar Oatmeal Raisin Bar Mix
3/4 C. butter or margarine,
  softened

1 egg, slightly beaten
1 tsp. vanilla

Preheat the oven to 350°F. In a large bowl, cream the butter, egg and vanilla. Add the Oatmeal Raisin Bar Mix and stir until the mixture is well blended. Spread batter into a lightly greased or sprayed 9 x 12 inch pan. Bake for 25 to 30 minutes. Cool in pan. Cut into 2-inch squares.

Oatmeal Raisin Bars
Makes 24 bars

1 jar Oatmeal Raisin Bar Mix
3/4 C. butter or margarine,
  softened

1 egg, slightly beaten
1 tsp. vanilla

Preheat the oven to 350°F. In a large bowl, cream the butter, egg and vanilla. Add the Oatmeal Raisin Bar Mix and stir until the mixture is well blended. Spread batter into a lightly greased or sprayed 9 x 12 inch pan. Bake for 25 to 30 minutes. Cool in pan. Cut into 2-inch squares.

Oatmeal Raisin Bars
Makes 24 bars

1 jar Oatmeal Raisin Bar Mix
3/4 C. butter or margarine,
  softened

1 egg, slightly beaten
1 tsp. vanilla

Preheat the oven to 350°F. In a large bowl, cream the butter, egg and vanilla. Add the Oatmeal Raisin Bar Mix and stir until the mixture is well blended. Spread batter into a lightly greased or sprayed 9 x 12 inch pan. Bake for 25 to 30 minutes. Cool in pan. Cut into 2-inch squares.

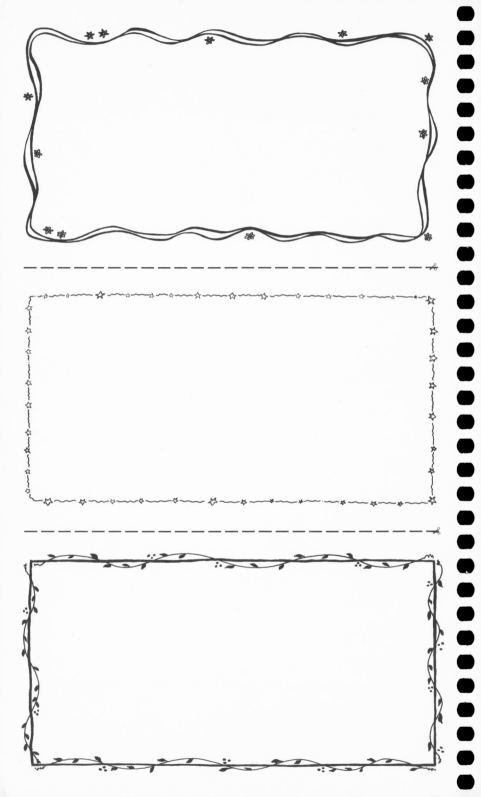

Hawaiian Bar Mix

1/3 C. sugar
1/2 C. brown sugar
1/3 C. flaked coconut
2/3 C. chopped macadamia
    nuts
2/3 C. chopped dates
2 C. all-purpose flour
1 tsp. baking soda
1 tsp. baking powder

Layer the ingredients in the order given into a wide-mouth 1-quart canning jar. Pack each layer in place before adding the next ingredient.

Attach a gift tag with the mixing and baking directions.

Hawaiian Bars

Makes 24 bars

1 jar Hawaiian Bar Mix
3/4 C. butter or margarine,
  softened
2 eggs, slightly beaten
2 tsp. vanilla

Preheat the oven to 350°F. In a large bowl, cream the butter, eggs and vanilla. Add the Hawaiian Bar Mix and stir until the mixture is well blended. Spread batter into a lightly greased or sprayed 9 x 12 inch pan. Bake for 25 to 30 minutes. Cool in pan. Cut into 2-inch squares.

Hawaiian Bars
Makes 24 bars

1 jar Hawaiian Bar Mix
3/4 C. butter or margarine,
  softened

2 eggs, slightly beaten
2 tsp. vanilla

    Preheat the oven to 350°F. In a large bowl, cream the butter, eggs and vanilla. Add the Hawaiian Bar Mix and stir until the mixture is well blended. Spread batter into a lightly greased or sprayed 9 x 12 inch pan. Bake for 25 to 30 minutes. Cool in pan. Cut into 2-inch squares.

Hawaiian Bars
Makes 24 bars

1 jar Hawaiian Bar Mix
3/4 C. butter or margarine,
  softened

2 eggs, slightly beaten
2 tsp. vanilla

    Preheat the oven to 350°F. In a large bowl, cream the butter, eggs and vanilla. Add the Hawaiian Bar Mix and stir until the mixture is well blended. Spread batter into a lightly greased or sprayed 9 x 12 inch pan. Bake for 25 to 30 minutes. Cool in pan. Cut into 2-inch squares.

Hawaiian Bars
Makes 24 bars

1 jar Hawaiian Bar Mix
3/4 C. butter or margarine,
  softened

2 eggs, slightly beaten
2 tsp. vanilla

    Preheat the oven to 350°F. In a large bowl, cream the butter, eggs and vanilla. Add the Hawaiian Bar Mix and stir until the mixture is well blended. Spread batter into a lightly greased or sprayed 9 x 12 inch pan. Bake for 25 to 30 minutes. Cool in pan. Cut into 2-inch squares.

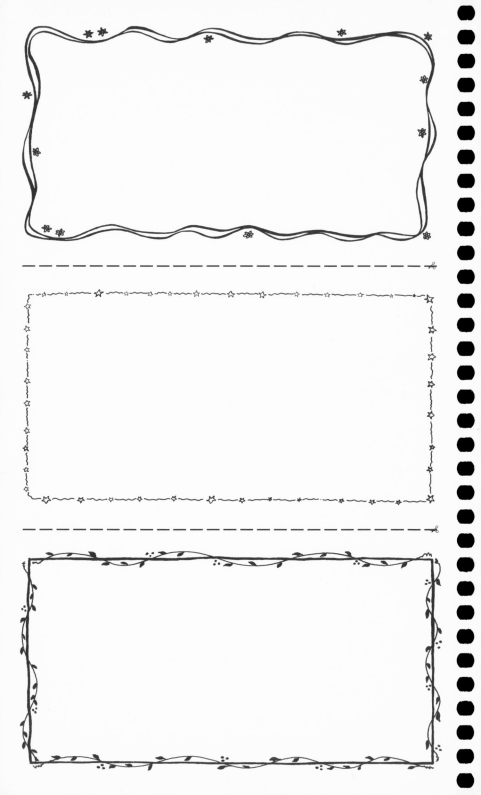

Hawaiian Bars
Makes 24 bars

1 jar Hawaiian Bar Mix
3/4 C. butter or margarine,
   softened

2 eggs, slightly beaten
2 tsp. vanilla

Preheat the oven to 350°F. In a large bowl, cream the butter, eggs and vanilla. Add the Hawaiian Bar Mix and stir until the mixture is well blended. Spread batter into a lightly greased or sprayed 9 x 12 inch pan. Bake for 25 to 30 minutes. Cool in pan. Cut into 2-inch squares.

Hawaiian Bars
Makes 24 bars

1 jar Hawaiian Bar Mix
3/4 C. butter or margarine,
   softened

2 eggs, slightly beaten
2 tsp. vanilla

Preheat the oven to 350°F. In a large bowl, cream the butter, eggs and vanilla. Add the Hawaiian Bar Mix and stir until the mixture is well blended. Spread batter into a lightly greased or sprayed 9 x 12 inch pan. Bake for 25 to 30 minutes. Cool in pan. Cut into 2-inch squares.

Hawaiian Bars
Makes 24 bars

1 jar Hawaiian Bar Mix
3/4 C. butter or margarine,
   softened

2 eggs, slightly beaten
2 tsp. vanilla

Preheat the oven to 350°F. In a large bowl, cream the butter, eggs and vanilla. Add the Hawaiian Bar Mix and stir until the mixture is well blended. Spread batter into a lightly greased or sprayed 9 x 12 inch pan. Bake for 25 to 30 minutes. Cool in pan. Cut into 2-inch squares.

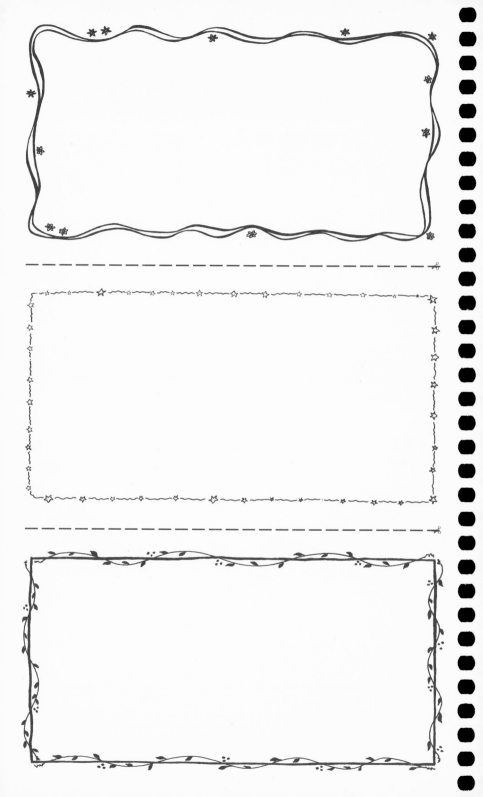

Chocolate-Macadamia Nut Bar Mix

1 1/4 C. sugar
1/2 C. chopped macadamia nuts
1 C. chocolate chips
2 C. all-purpose flour
1/2 tsp. baking soda
1/2 tsp. baking powder

Layer the ingredients in the order given into a wide-mouth 1-quart canning jar. Pack each layer in place before adding the next ingredient.

Attach a gift tag with the mixing and baking directions.

❁ *To make a gift in a jar fancier, decorate it with a doily and ribbon.* ❁

Chocolate-Macadamia Nut Bars

Makes 24 bars

1 jar White Chocolate-
  Macadamia Nut Bar Mix
1 C. butter or margarine,
  softened
2 eggs, slightly beaten
2 tsp. vanilla

Preheat the oven to 375°F. In a large bowl, cream the butter, eggs and vanilla. Add the White Chocolate-Macadamia Nut Bar Mix and stir until the mixture is well blended. Spread batter into a lightly greased or sprayed 9 x 12 inch pan. Bake for 25 to 30 minutes. Cool in pan. Cut into 2-inch squares.

Chocolate-Macadamia Nut Bars
Makes 24 bars

1 jar White Chocolate-
Macadamia Nut Bar Mix
1 C. butter or margarine,
softened

2 eggs, slightly beaten
2 tsp. vanilla

Preheat the oven to 375°F. In a large bowl, cream the butter, eggs and vanilla. Add the White Chocolate-Macadamia Nut Bar Mix and stir until the mixture is well blended. Spread batter into a lightly greased or sprayed 9 x 12 inch pan. Bake for 25 to 30 minutes. Cool in pan. Cut into 2-inch squares.

Chocolate-Macadamia Nut Bars
Makes 24 bars

1 jar White Chocolate-
Macadamia Nut Bar Mix
1 C. butter or margarine,
softened

2 eggs, slightly beaten
2 tsp. vanilla

Preheat the oven to 375°F. In a large bowl, cream the butter, eggs and vanilla. Add the White Chocolate-Macadamia Nut Bar Mix and stir until the mixture is well blended. Spread batter into a lightly greased or sprayed 9 x 12 inch pan. Bake for 25 to 30 minutes. Cool in pan. Cut into 2-inch squares.

Chocolate-Macadamia Nut Bars
Makes 24 bars

1 jar White Chocolate-
Macadamia Nut Bar Mix
1 C. butter or margarine,
softened

2 eggs, slightly beaten
2 tsp. vanilla

Preheat the oven to 375°F. In a large bowl, cream the butter, eggs and vanilla. Add the White Chocolate-Macadamia Nut Bar Mix and stir until the mixture is well blended. Spread batter into a lightly greased or sprayed 9 x 12 inch pan. Bake for 25 to 30 minutes. Cool in pan. Cut into 2-inch squares.

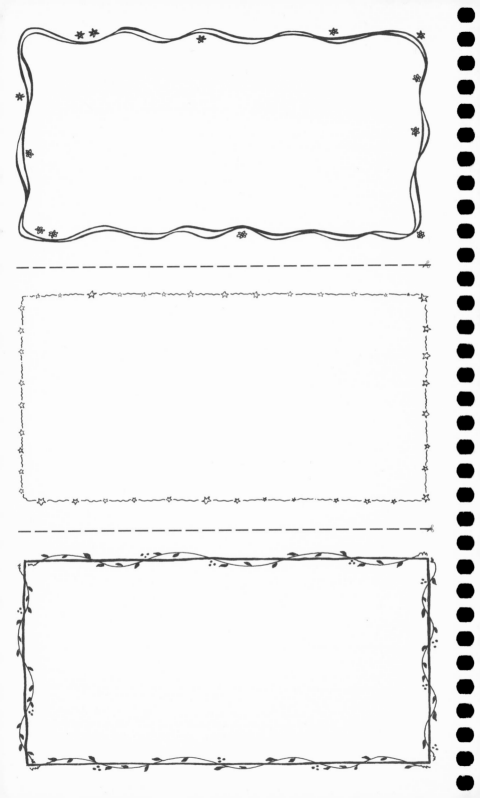

Chocolate-Macadamia Nut Bars
Makes 24 bars

1 jar White Chocolate-
  Macadamia Nut Bar Mix
1 C. butter or margarine,
  softened

2 eggs, slightly beaten
2 tsp. vanilla

Preheat the oven to 375°F. In a large bowl, cream the butter, eggs and vanilla. Add the White Chocolate-Macadamia Nut Bar Mix and stir until the mixture is well blended. Spread batter into a lightly greased or sprayed 9 x 12 inch pan. Bake for 25 to 30 minutes. Cool in pan. Cut into 2-inch squares.

Chocolate-Macadamia Nut Bars
Makes 24 bars

1 jar White Chocolate-
  Macadamia Nut Bar Mix
1 C. butter or margarine,
  softened

2 eggs, slightly beaten
2 tsp. vanilla

Preheat the oven to 375°F. In a large bowl, cream the butter, eggs and vanilla. Add the White Chocolate-Macadamia Nut Bar Mix and stir until the mixture is well blended. Spread batter into a lightly greased or sprayed 9 x 12 inch pan. Bake for 25 to 30 minutes. Cool in pan. Cut into 2-inch squares.

Chocolate-Macadamia Nut Bars
Makes 24 bars

1 jar White Chocolate-
  Macadamia Nut Bar Mix
1 C. butter or margarine,
  softened

2 eggs, slightly beaten
2 tsp. vanilla

Preheat the oven to 375°F. In a large bowl, cream the butter, eggs and vanilla. Add the White Chocolate-Macadamia Nut Bar Mix and stir until the mixture is well blended. Spread batter into a lightly greased or sprayed 9 x 12 inch pan. Bake for 25 to 30 minutes. Cool in pan. Cut into 2-inch squares.

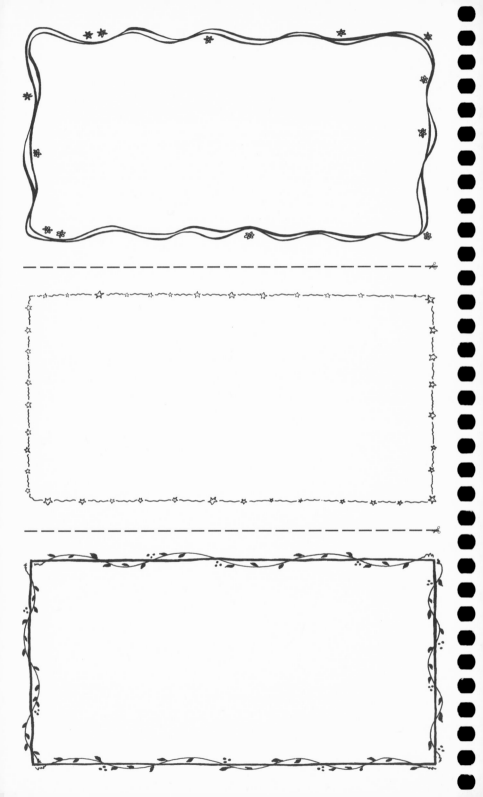

Chunky Chocolate Bar Mix

3/4 C. brown sugar
1/2 C. sugar
1/4 C. cocoa powder (clean
    inside of jar with a paper
    towel after this layer)
1/2 C. chopped pecans
1 C. jumbo chocolate chips
1 3/4 C. all-purpose flour
1 tsp. baking soda
1 tsp. baking powder
1/4 tsp. salt

    Layer the ingredients in the order given into a wide-mouth 1-quart canning jar. Pack each layer in place before adding the next ingredient.

    Attach a gift tag with the mixing and baking directions.

❀ *For a special touch, attach a wooden spoon to the jar.* ❀

Chunky Chocolate Bars

Makes 24 bars

1 jar Chunky Chocolate Bar Mix
3/4 C. butter or margarine,
  softened
3 eggs, slightly beaten
1 tsp. vanilla

Preheat the oven to 350°F. In a large bowl, cream the butter, eggs and vanilla. Add the Chunky Chocolate Bar Mix and stir until the mixture is well blended. Spread batter into a lightly greased or sprayed 9 x 12 inch pan. Bake for 30 to 35 minutes. Cool in pan. Cut into 2-inch squares.

Chunky Chocolate Bars
Makes 24 bars

1 jar Chunky Chocolate Bar Mix
3/4 C. butter or margarine,
   softened

3 eggs, slightly beaten
1 tsp. vanilla

    Preheat the oven to 350°F. In a large bowl, cream the butter, eggs and vanilla. Add the Chunky Chocolate Bar Mix and stir until the mixture is well blended. Spread batter into a lightly greased or sprayed 9 x 12 inch pan. Bake for 30 to 35 minutes. Cool in pan. Cut into 2-inch squares.

Chunky Chocolate Bars
Makes 24 bars

1 jar Chunky Chocolate Bar Mix
3/4 C. butter or margarine,
   softened

3 eggs, slightly beaten
1 tsp. vanilla

    Preheat the oven to 350°F. In a large bowl, cream the butter, eggs and vanilla. Add the Chunky Chocolate Bar Mix and stir until the mixture is well blended. Spread batter into a lightly greased or sprayed 9 x 12 inch pan. Bake for 30 to 35 minutes. Cool in pan. Cut into 2-inch squares.

Chunky Chocolate Bars
Makes 24 bars

1 jar Chunky Chocolate Bar Mix
3/4 C. butter or margarine,
   softened

3 eggs, slightly beaten
1 tsp. vanilla

    Preheat the oven to 350°F. In a large bowl, cream the butter, eggs and vanilla. Add the Chunky Chocolate Bar Mix and stir until the mixture is well blended. Spread batter into a lightly greased or sprayed 9 x 12 inch pan. Bake for 30 to 35 minutes. Cool in pan. Cut into 2-inch squares.

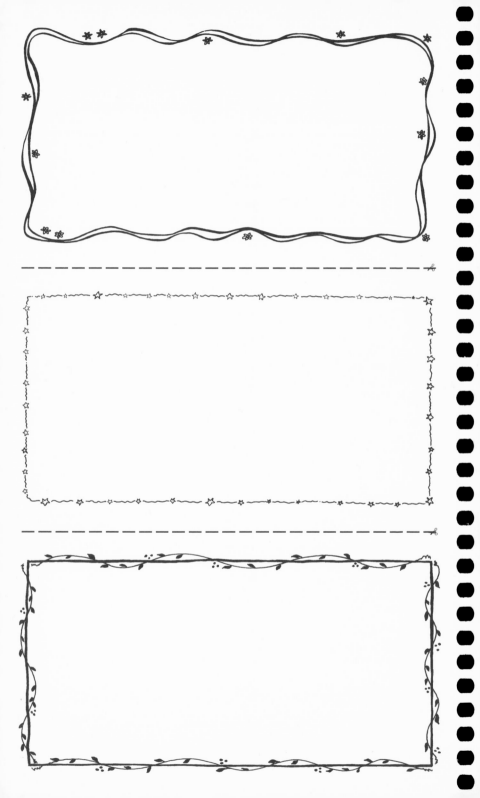

Chunky Chocolate Bars
Makes 24 bars

1 jar Chunky Chocolate Bar Mix
3/4 C. butter or margarine,
  softened

3 eggs, slightly beaten
1 tsp. vanilla

    Preheat the oven to 350°F. In a large bowl, cream the butter, eggs and vanilla. Add the Chunky Chocolate Bar Mix and stir until the mixture is well blended. Spread batter into a lightly greased or sprayed 9 x 12 inch pan. Bake for 30 to 35 minutes. Cool in pan. Cut into 2-inch squares.

Chunky Chocolate Bars
Makes 24 bars

1 jar Chunky Chocolate Bar Mix
3/4 C. butter or margarine,
  softened

3 eggs, slightly beaten
1 tsp. vanilla

    Preheat the oven to 350°F. In a large bowl, cream the butter, eggs and vanilla. Add the Chunky Chocolate Bar Mix and stir until the mixture is well blended. Spread batter into a lightly greased or sprayed 9 x 12 inch pan. Bake for 30 to 35 minutes. Cool in pan. Cut into 2-inch squares.

Chunky Chocolate Bars
Makes 24 bars

1 jar Chunky Chocolate Bar Mix
3/4 C. butter or margarine,
  softened

3 eggs, slightly beaten
1 tsp. vanilla

    Preheat the oven to 350°F. In a large bowl, cream the butter, eggs and vanilla. Add the Chunky Chocolate Bar Mix and stir until the mixture is well blended. Spread batter into a lightly greased or sprayed 9 x 12 inch pan. Bake for 30 to 35 minutes. Cool in pan. Cut into 2-inch squares.

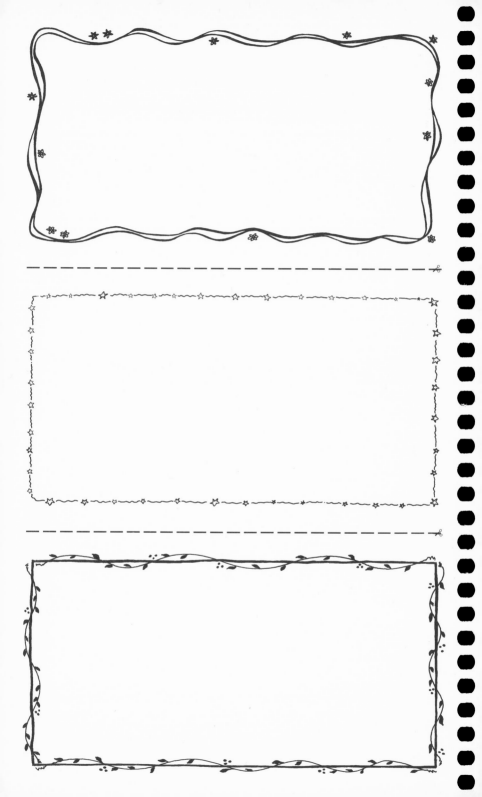

Gourmet Bar Mix

1 C. all-purpose flour
1/2 tsp. baking powder
1/2 tsp. baking soda
1 1/4 C. old-fashioned oats, blended
1 (5.5 ounce) milk chocolate bar, grated
1/2 C. sugar
1/2 C. brown sugar
1/2 C. chopped nuts, your choice (optional)
1/2 C. chocolate chips

Layer the ingredients in the order given into a wide-mouth 1-quart canning jar. Pack each layer in place before adding the next ingredient.

Attach a gift tag with the mixing and baking directions.

Gourmet Bars

Makes 24 bars

1 jar Gourmet Bar Mix
1/2 C. butter or margarine,
   softened
2 eggs, slightly beaten
1 T. milk
1 tsp. vanilla

Preheat the oven to 350°F. In a large bowl, cream the butter, eggs, milk and vanilla. Add the Gourmet Bar Mix and stir until the mixture is well blended. Spread batter into a lightly greased or sprayed 9 x 12 inch pan. Bake for 20 to 25 minutes. Cool in pan. Cut into 2-inch squares.

Gourmet Bars
Makes 24 bars

1 jar Gourmet Bar Mix
1/2 C. butter or margarine,
  softened

2 eggs, slightly beaten
1 T. milk
1 tsp. vanilla

    Preheat the oven to 350°F. In a large bowl, cream the butter, eggs, milk and vanilla. Add the Gourmet Bar Mix and stir until the mixture is well blended. Spread batter into a lightly greased or sprayed 9 x 12 inch pan. Bake for 20 to 25 minutes. Cool in pan. Cut into 2-inch squares.

Gourmet Bars
Makes 24 bars

1 jar Gourmet Bar Mix
1/2 C. butter or margarine,
  softened

2 eggs, slightly beaten
1 T. milk
1 tsp. vanilla

    Preheat the oven to 350°F. In a large bowl, cream the butter, eggs, milk and vanilla. Add the Gourmet Bar Mix and stir until the mixture is well blended. Spread batter into a lightly greased or sprayed 9 x 12 inch pan. Bake for 20 to 25 minutes. Cool in pan. Cut into 2-inch squares.

Gourmet Bars
Makes 24 bars

1 jar Gourmet Bar Mix
1/2 C. butter or margarine,
  softened

2 eggs, slightly beaten
1 T. milk
1 tsp. vanilla

    Preheat the oven to 350°F. In a large bowl, cream the butter, eggs, milk and vanilla. Add the Gourmet Bar Mix and stir until the mixture is well blended. Spread batter into a lightly greased or sprayed 9 x 12 inch pan. Bake for 20 to 25 minutes. Cool in pan. Cut into 2-inch squares.

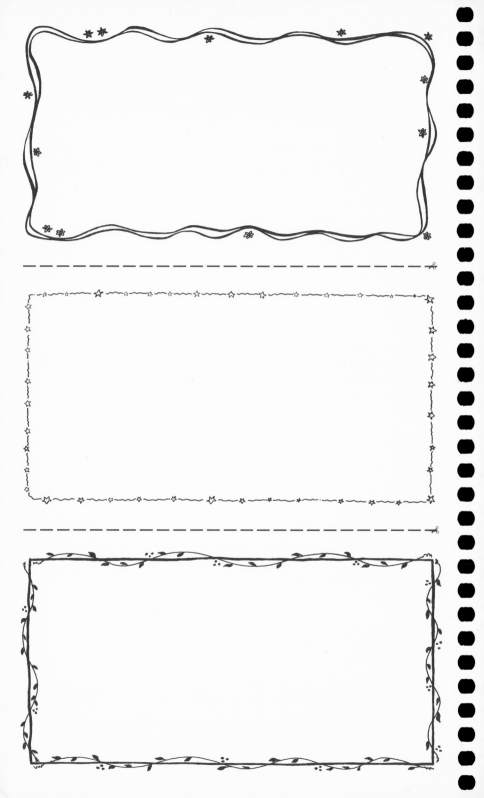

Gourmet Bars
Makes 24 bars

1 jar Gourmet Bar Mix
1/2 C. butter or margarine,
  softened

2 eggs, slightly beaten
1 T. milk
1 tsp. vanilla

Preheat the oven to 350°F. In a large bowl, cream the butter, eggs, milk and vanilla. Add the Gourmet Bar Mix and stir until the mixture is well blended. Spread batter into a lightly greased or sprayed 9 x 12 inch pan. Bake for 20 to 25 minutes. Cool in pan. Cut into 2-inch squares.

Gourmet Bars
Makes 24 bars

1 jar Gourmet Bar Mix
1/2 C. butter or margarine,
  softened

2 eggs, slightly beaten
1 T. milk
1 tsp. vanilla

Preheat the oven to 350°F. In a large bowl, cream the butter, eggs, milk and vanilla. Add the Gourmet Bar Mix and stir until the mixture is well blended. Spread batter into a lightly greased or sprayed 9 x 12 inch pan. Bake for 20 to 25 minutes. Cool in pan. Cut into 2-inch squares.

Gourmet Bars
Makes 24 bars

1 jar Gourmet Bar Mix
1/2 C. butter or margarine,
  softened

2 eggs, slightly beaten
1 T. milk
1 tsp. vanilla

Preheat the oven to 350°F. In a large bowl, cream the butter, eggs, milk and vanilla. Add the Gourmet Bar Mix and stir until the mixture is well blended. Spread batter into a lightly greased or sprayed 9 x 12 inch pan. Bake for 20 to 25 minutes. Cool in pan. Cut into 2-inch squares.

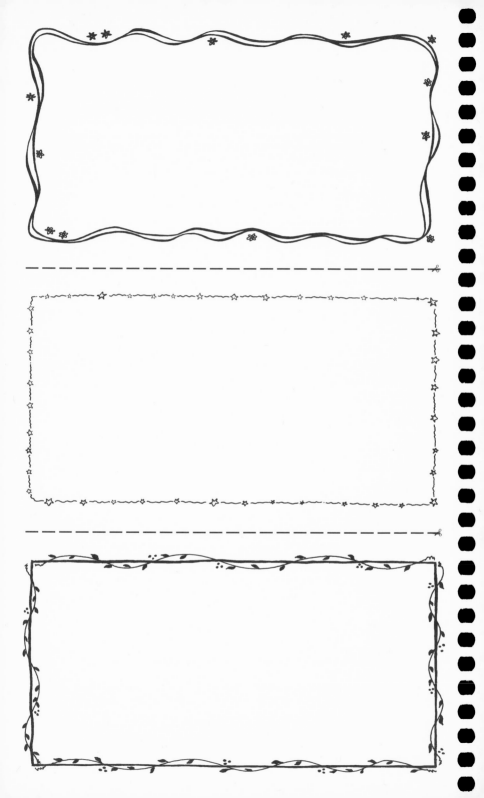

Peanut Butter Chocolate Chip Bar Mix

3/4 C. sugar
3/4 C. brown sugar
1 C. chocolate chips
2 C. all-purpose flour
1/2 tsp. baking soda
1/4 tsp. salt

Layer the ingredients in the order given into a wide-mouth 1-quart canning jar. Pack each layer in place before adding the next ingredient.

Attach a gift tag with the mixing and baking directions.

❀ Small appliques or embroidery can be added to the center of a fabric cover to further personalize the gift. ❀

Peanut Butter Chocolate Chip Bars

Makes 24 bars

1 jar Peanut Butter Chocolate
  Chip Bar Mix
1 C. butter or margarine,
  softened
2 eggs, slightly beaten
2 tsp. vanilla
1 C. creamy peanut butter

Preheat the oven to 350°F. In a large bowl, cream the butter, eggs and vanilla. Blend in the peanut butter. Add the Peanut Butter Chocolate Chip Bar Mix and stir until the mixture is well blended. Spread batter into a lightly greased or sprayed 9 x 12 inch pan. Bake for 30 to 35 minutes. Cool in pan. Cut into 2-inch squares.

Peanut Butter Chocolate Chip Bars
Makes 24 bars

1 jar Peanut Butter Chocolate
  Chip Bar Mix
1 C. butter or margarine,
  softened

2 eggs, slightly beaten
2 tsp. vanilla
1 C. creamy peanut butter

Preheat the oven to 350°F. In a large bowl, cream the butter, eggs and vanilla. Blend in the peanut butter. Add the Peanut Butter Chocolate Chip Bar Mix and stir until the mixture is well blended. Spread batter into a lightly greased or sprayed 9 x 12 inch pan. Bake for 30 to 35 minutes. Cool in pan. Cut into 2-inch squares.

Peanut Butter Chocolate Chip Bars
Makes 24 bars

1 jar Peanut Butter Chocolate
  Chip Bar Mix
1 C. butter or margarine,
  softened

2 eggs, slightly beaten
2 tsp. vanilla
1 C. creamy peanut butter

Preheat the oven to 350°F. In a large bowl, cream the butter, eggs and vanilla. Blend in the peanut butter. Add the Peanut Butter Chocolate Chip Bar Mix and stir until the mixture is well blended. Spread batter into a lightly greased or sprayed 9 x 12 inch pan. Bake for 30 to 35 minutes. Cool in pan. Cut into 2-inch squares.

Peanut Butter Chocolate Chip Bars
Makes 24 bars

1 jar Peanut Butter Chocolate
  Chip Bar Mix
1 C. butter or margarine,
  softened

2 eggs, slightly beaten
2 tsp. vanilla
1 C. creamy peanut butter

Preheat the oven to 350°F. In a large bowl, cream the butter, eggs and vanilla. Blend in the peanut butter. Add the Peanut Butter Chocolate Chip Bar Mix and stir until the mixture is well blended. Spread batter into a lightly greased or sprayed 9 x 12 inch pan. Bake for 30 to 35 minutes. Cool in pan. Cut into 2-inch squares.

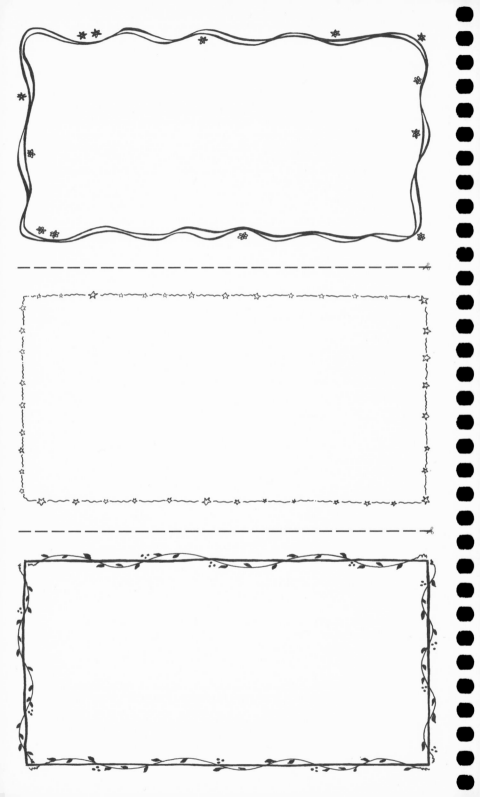

Peanut Butter Chocolate Chip Bars
Makes 24 bars

1 jar Peanut Butter Chocolate
  Chip Bar Mix
1 C. butter or margarine,
  softened

2 eggs, slightly beaten
2 tsp. vanilla
1 C. creamy peanut butter

    Preheat the oven to 350°F. In a large bowl, cream the butter, eggs and vanilla. Blend in the peanut butter. Add the Peanut Butter Chocolate Chip Bar Mix and stir until the mixture is well blended. Spread batter into a lightly greased or sprayed 9 x 12 inch pan. Bake for 30 to 35 minutes. Cool in pan. Cut into 2-inch squares.

Peanut Butter Chocolate Chip Bars
Makes 24 bars

1 jar Peanut Butter Chocolate
  Chip Bar Mix
1 C. butter or margarine,
  softened

2 eggs, slightly beaten
2 tsp. vanilla
1 C. creamy peanut butter

    Preheat the oven to 350°F. In a large bowl, cream the butter, eggs and vanilla. Blend in the peanut butter. Add the Peanut Butter Chocolate Chip Bar Mix and stir until the mixture is well blended. Spread batter into a lightly greased or sprayed 9 x 12 inch pan. Bake for 30 to 35 minutes. Cool in pan. Cut into 2-inch squares.

Peanut Butter Chocolate Chip Bars
Makes 24 bars

1 jar Peanut Butter Chocolate
  Chip Bar Mix
1 C. butter or margarine,
  softened

2 eggs, slightly beaten
2 tsp. vanilla
1 C. creamy peanut butter

    Preheat the oven to 350°F. In a large bowl, cream the butter, eggs and vanilla. Blend in the peanut butter. Add the Peanut Butter Chocolate Chip Bar Mix and stir until the mixture is well blended. Spread batter into a lightly greased or sprayed 9 x 12 inch pan. Bake for 30 to 35 minutes. Cool in pan. Cut into 2-inch squares.

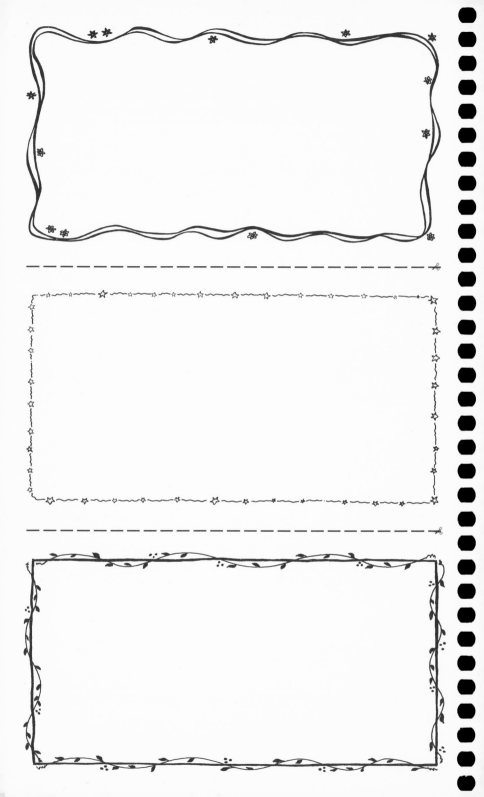

Pecan Bar Mix

3/4 C. old-fashioned oats
1/4 C. brown sugar
1/2 C. chopped pecans
1/4 C. brown sugar
1 C. crisped rice cereal
3/4 C. all-purpose flour
1/2 tsp. baking soda
1/2 tsp. baking powder
1/2 C. sugar

Layer the ingredients in the order given into a wide-mouth 1-quart canning jar. Pack each layer in place before adding the next ingredient.

Attach a gift tag with the mixing and baking directions.

Pecan Bars

Makes 24 bars

1 jar Pecan Bar Mix
1/2 C. butter or margarine,
    softened
2 eggs, slightly beaten
1 tsp. vanilla

Preheat the oven to 350°F. In a large bowl, cream the butter, eggs and vanilla. Add the Pecan Bar Mix and stir until the mixture is well blended. Spread batter into a lightly greased or sprayed 9 x 12 inch pan. Bake for 20 to 25 minutes. Cool in pan. Cut into 2-inch squares.

Pecan Bars
Makes 24 bars

1 jar Pecan Bar Mix
1/2 C. butter or margarine,
  softened

2 eggs, slightly beaten
1 tsp. vanilla

Preheat the oven to 350°F. In a large bowl, cream the butter, eggs and vanilla. Add the Pecan Bar Mix and stir until the mixture is well blended. Spread batter into a lightly greased or sprayed 9 x 12 inch pan. Bake for 20 to 25 minutes. Cool in pan. Cut into 2-inch squares.

Pecan Bars
Makes 24 bars

1 jar Pecan Bar Mix
1/2 C. butter or margarine,
  softened

2 eggs, slightly beaten
1 tsp. vanilla

Preheat the oven to 350°F. In a large bowl, cream the butter, eggs and vanilla. Add the Pecan Bar Mix and stir until the mixture is well blended. Spread batter into a lightly greased or sprayed 9 x 12 inch pan. Bake for 20 to 25 minutes. Cool in pan. Cut into 2-inch squares.

Pecan Bars
Makes 24 bars

1 jar Pecan Bar Mix
1/2 C. butter or margarine,
  softened

2 eggs, slightly beaten
1 tsp. vanilla

Preheat the oven to 350°F. In a large bowl, cream the butter, eggs and vanilla. Add the Pecan Bar Mix and stir until the mixture is well blended. Spread batter into a lightly greased or sprayed 9 x 12 inch pan. Bake for 20 to 25 minutes. Cool in pan. Cut into 2-inch squares.

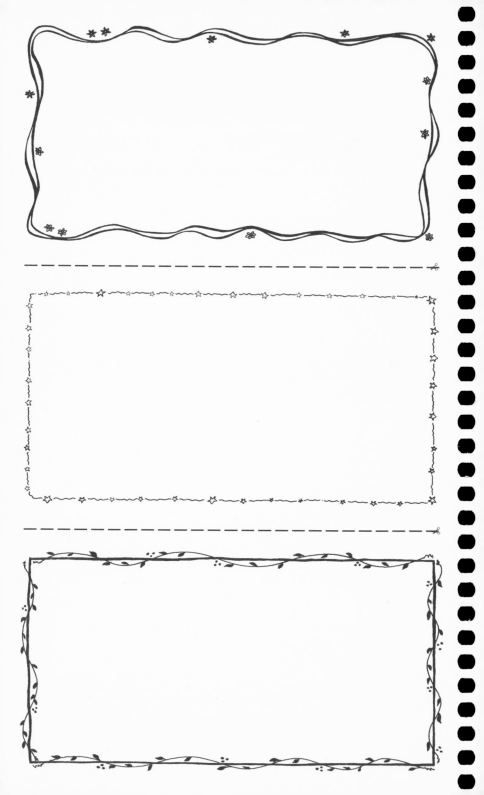

Pecan Bars
Makes 24 bars

1 jar Pecan Bar Mix
1/2 C. butter or margarine,
    softened

2 eggs, slightly beaten
1 tsp. vanilla

   Preheat the oven to 350°F. In a large bowl, cream the butter, eggs and vanilla. Add the Pecan Bar Mix and stir until the mixture is well blended. Spread batter into a lightly greased or sprayed 9 x 12 inch pan. Bake for 20 to 25 minutes. Cool in pan. Cut into 2-inch squares.

Pecan Bars
Makes 24 bars

1 jar Pecan Bar Mix
1/2 C. butter or margarine,
    softened

2 eggs, slightly beaten
1 tsp. vanilla

   Preheat the oven to 350°F. In a large bowl, cream the butter, eggs and vanilla. Add the Pecan Bar Mix and stir until the mixture is well blended. Spread batter into a lightly greased or sprayed 9 x 12 inch pan. Bake for 20 to 25 minutes. Cool in pan. Cut into 2-inch squares.

Pecan Bars
Makes 24 bars

1 jar Pecan Bar Mix
1/2 C. butter or margarine,
    softened

2 eggs, slightly beaten
1 tsp. vanilla

   Preheat the oven to 350°F. In a large bowl, cream the butter, eggs and vanilla. Add the Pecan Bar Mix and stir until the mixture is well blended. Spread batter into a lightly greased or sprayed 9 x 12 inch pan. Bake for 20 to 25 minutes. Cool in pan. Cut into 2-inch squares.

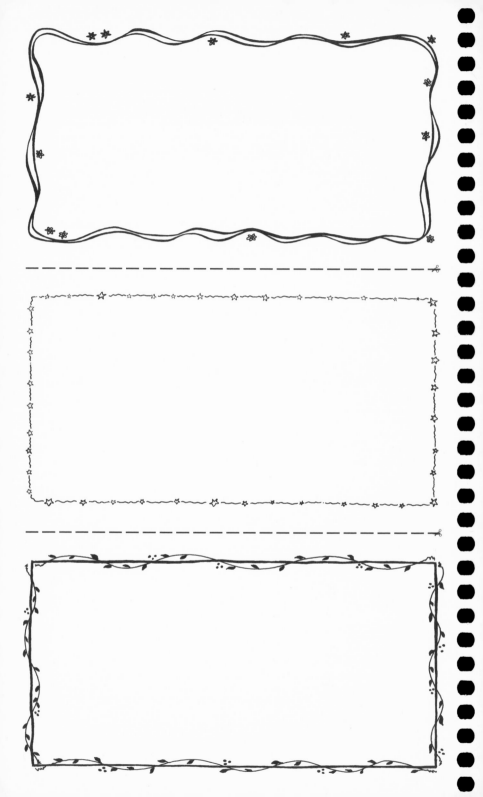

Raisin Nutty Spice Bar Mix

3/4 C. golden raisins
1 C. salted peanuts, chopped
2 C. all-purpose flour
1 tsp. baking soda
1 tsp. baking powder
1 tsp. allspice
3/4 C. sugar

Layer the ingredients in the order given into a wide-mouth 1-quart canning jar. Pack each layer in place before adding the next ingredient.

Attach a gift tag with the mixing and baking directions.

❀ *For a different look, place a small amount of stuffing under a fabric cover before attaching to "puff" the top.* ❀

Raisin Nutty Spice Bars

Makes 24 bars

1 jar Raisin Nutty Spice
   Bar Mix
3/4 C. butter or margarine,
   softened
2 eggs, slightly beaten
1/4 C. milk
1 tsp. vanilla

Preheat the oven to 375°F. In a large bowl, cream the butter, eggs, milk and vanilla. Add the Raisin Nutty Spice Bar Mix and stir until the mixture is well blended. Spread batter into a lightly greased or sprayed 9 x 12 inch pan. Bake for 15 to 20 minutes. Cool in pan. Cut into 2-inch squares.

Raisin Nutty Spice Bars
Makes 24 bars

1 jar Raisin Nutty Spice Bar Mix   2 eggs, slightly beaten
3/4 C. butter or margarine,   1/4 C. milk
   softened   1 tsp. vanilla

    Preheat the oven to 375°F. In a large bowl, cream the butter, eggs, milk and vanilla. Add the Raisin Nutty Spice Bar Mix and stir until the mixture is well blended. Spread batter into a lightly greased or sprayed 9 x 12 inch pan. Bake for 15 to 20 minutes. Cool in pan. Cut into 2-inch squares.

Raisin Nutty Spice Bars
Makes 24 bars

1 jar Raisin Nutty Spice Bar Mix   2 eggs, slightly beaten
3/4 C. butter or margarine,   1/4 C. milk
   softened   1 tsp. vanilla

    Preheat the oven to 375°F. In a large bowl, cream the butter, eggs, milk and vanilla. Add the Raisin Nutty Spice Bar Mix and stir until the mixture is well blended. Spread batter into a lightly greased or sprayed 9 x 12 inch pan. Bake for 15 to 20 minutes. Cool in pan. Cut into 2-inch squares.

Raisin Nutty Spice Bars
Makes 24 bars

1 jar Raisin Nutty Spice Bar Mix   2 eggs, slightly beaten
3/4 C. butter or margarine,   1/4 C. milk
   softened   1 tsp. vanilla

    Preheat the oven to 375°F. In a large bowl, cream the butter, eggs, milk and vanilla. Add the Raisin Nutty Spice Bar Mix and stir until the mixture is well blended. Spread batter into a lightly greased or sprayed 9 x 12 inch pan. Bake for 15 to 20 minutes. Cool in pan. Cut into 2-inch squares.

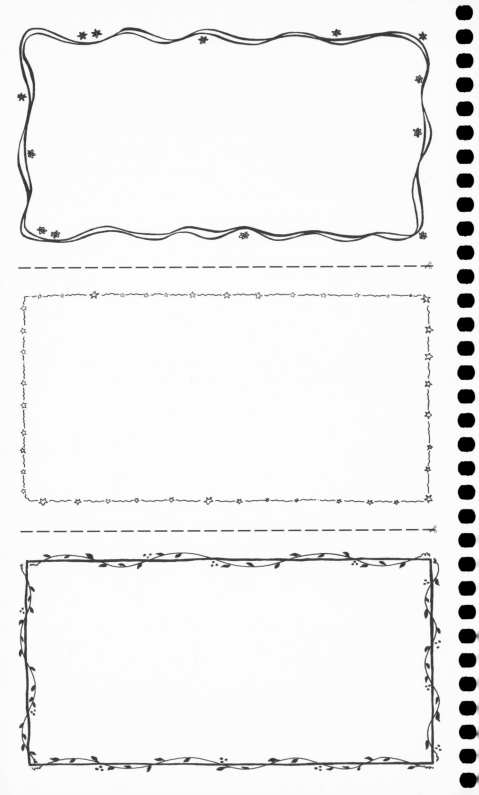

Raisin Nutty Spice Bars
Makes 24 bars

1 jar Raisin Nutty Spice Bar Mix
3/4 C. butter or margarine,
  softened

2 eggs, slightly beaten
1/4 C. milk
1 tsp. vanilla

Preheat the oven to 375°F. In a large bowl, cream the butter, eggs, milk and vanilla. Add the Raisin Nutty Spice Bar Mix and stir until the mixture is well blended. Spread batter into a lightly greased or sprayed 9 x 12 inch pan. Bake for 15 to 20 minutes. Cool in pan. Cut into 2-inch squares.

Raisin Nutty Spice Bars
Makes 24 bars

1 jar Raisin Nutty Spice Bar Mix
3/4 C. butter or margarine,
  softened

2 eggs, slightly beaten
1/4 C. milk
1 tsp. vanilla

Preheat the oven to 375°F. In a large bowl, cream the butter, eggs, milk and vanilla. Add the Raisin Nutty Spice Bar Mix and stir until the mixture is well blended. Spread batter into a lightly greased or sprayed 9 x 12 inch pan. Bake for 15 to 20 minutes. Cool in pan. Cut into 2-inch squares.

Raisin Nutty Spice Bars
Makes 24 bars

1 jar Raisin Nutty Spice Bar Mix
3/4 C. butter or margarine,
  softened

2 eggs, slightly beaten
1/4 C. milk
1 tsp. vanilla

Preheat the oven to 375°F. In a large bowl, cream the butter, eggs, milk and vanilla. Add the Raisin Nutty Spice Bar Mix and stir until the mixture is well blended. Spread batter into a lightly greased or sprayed 9 x 12 inch pan. Bake for 15 to 20 minutes. Cool in pan. Cut into 2-inch squares.

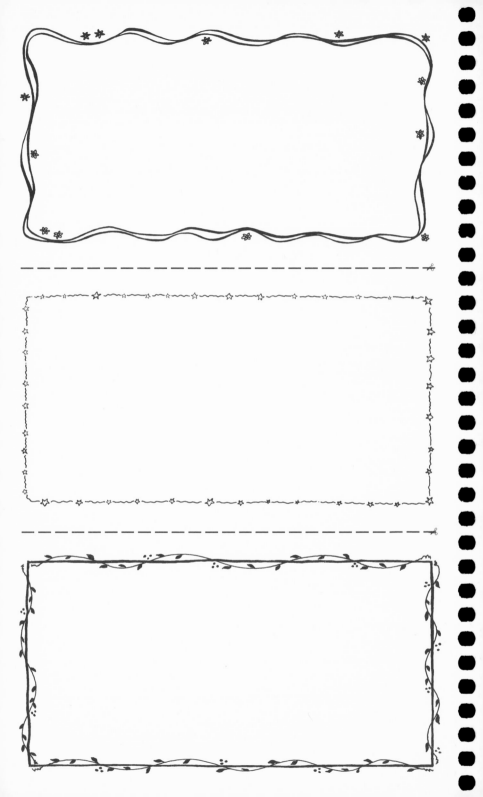

Peanut Butter Bar Mix

3/4 C. chopped salted peanuts
3/4 C. brown sugar
3/4 C. sugar
1 1/2 C. all-purpose flour
1 tsp. baking soda
1 tsp. salt
3/4 C. peanut butter chips

Layer the ingredients in the order given into a wide-mouth 1-quart canning jar. Pack each layer in place before adding the next ingredient.

Attach a gift tag with the mixing and baking directions.

Peanut Butter Bars

Makes 24 bars

1 jar Peanut Butter Bar Mix
1/2 C. butter or margarine,
   softened
1 egg, slightly beaten
1 tsp. vanilla
1/2 C. creamy peanut butter

Preheat the oven to 350°F. In a large bowl, cream the butter, egg and vanilla. Blend in the peanut butter. Add the Peanut Butter Bar Mix and stir until the mixture is well blended. Spread batter into a lightly greased or sprayed 9 x 12 inch pan. Bake for 25 to 30 minutes. Cool in pan. Cut into 2-inch squares.

Peanut Butter Bars
Makes 24 bars

1 jar Peanut Butter Bar Mix
1/2 C. butter or margarine,
  softened

1 egg, slightly beaten
1 tsp. vanilla
1/2 C. creamy peanut butter

    Preheat the oven to 350°F. In a large bowl, cream the butter, egg and vanilla. Blend in the peanut butter. Add the Peanut Butter Bar Mix and stir until the mixture is well blended. Spread batter into a lightly greased or sprayed 9 x 12 inch pan. Bake for 25 to 30 minutes. Cool in pan. Cut into 2-inch squares.

Peanut Butter Bars
Makes 24 bars

1 jar Peanut Butter Bar Mix
1/2 C. butter or margarine,
  softened

1 egg, slightly beaten
1 tsp. vanilla
1/2 C. creamy peanut butter

    Preheat the oven to 350°F. In a large bowl, cream the butter, egg and vanilla. Blend in the peanut butter. Add the Peanut Butter Bar Mix and stir until the mixture is well blended. Spread batter into a lightly greased or sprayed 9 x 12 inch pan. Bake for 25 to 30 minutes. Cool in pan. Cut into 2-inch squares.

Peanut Butter Bars
Makes 24 bars

1 jar Peanut Butter Bar Mix
1/2 C. butter or margarine,
  softened

1 egg, slightly beaten
1 tsp. vanilla
1/2 C. creamy peanut butter

    Preheat the oven to 350°F. In a large bowl, cream the butter, egg and vanilla. Blend in the peanut butter. Add the Peanut Butter Bar Mix and stir until the mixture is well blended. Spread batter into a lightly greased or sprayed 9 x 12 inch pan. Bake for 25 to 30 minutes. Cool in pan. Cut into 2-inch squares.

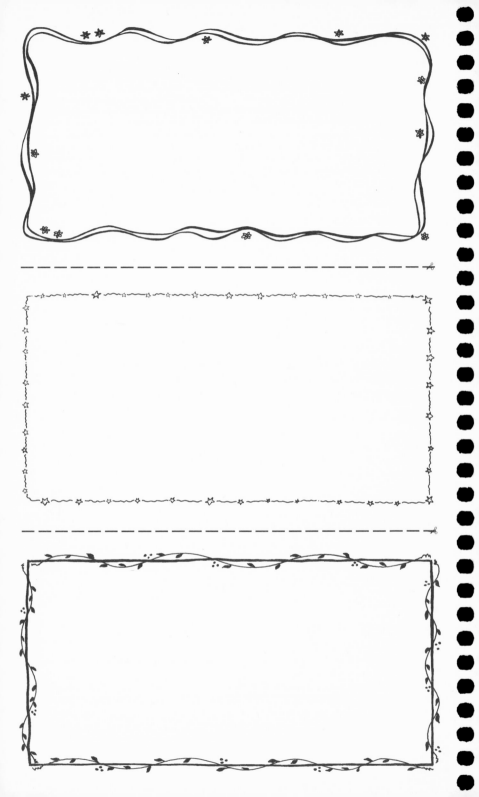

Peanut Butter Bars
Makes 24 bars

1 jar Peanut Butter Bar Mix
1/2 C. butter or margarine,
  softened

1 egg, slightly beaten
1 tsp. vanilla
1/2 C. creamy peanut butter

    Preheat the oven to 350°F. In a large bowl, cream the butter, egg and vanilla. Blend in the peanut butter. Add the Peanut Butter Bar Mix and stir until the mixture is well blended. Spread batter into a lightly greased or sprayed 9 x 12 inch pan. Bake for 25 to 30 minutes. Cool in pan. Cut into 2-inch squares.

Peanut Butter Bars
Makes 24 bars

1 jar Peanut Butter Bar Mix
1/2 C. butter or margarine,
  softened

1 egg, slightly beaten
1 tsp. vanilla
1/2 C. creamy peanut butter

    Preheat the oven to 350°F. In a large bowl, cream the butter, egg and vanilla. Blend in the peanut butter. Add the Peanut Butter Bar Mix and stir until the mixture is well blended. Spread batter into a lightly greased or sprayed 9 x 12 inch pan. Bake for 25 to 30 minutes. Cool in pan. Cut into 2-inch squares.

Peanut Butter Bars
Makes 24 bars

1 jar Peanut Butter Bar Mix
1/2 C. butter or margarine,
  softened

1 egg, slightly beaten
1 tsp. vanilla
1/2 C. creamy peanut butter

    Preheat the oven to 350°F. In a large bowl, cream the butter, egg and vanilla. Blend in the peanut butter. Add the Peanut Butter Bar Mix and stir until the mixture is well blended. Spread batter into a lightly greased or sprayed 9 x 12 inch pan. Bake for 25 to 30 minutes. Cool in pan. Cut into 2-inch squares.

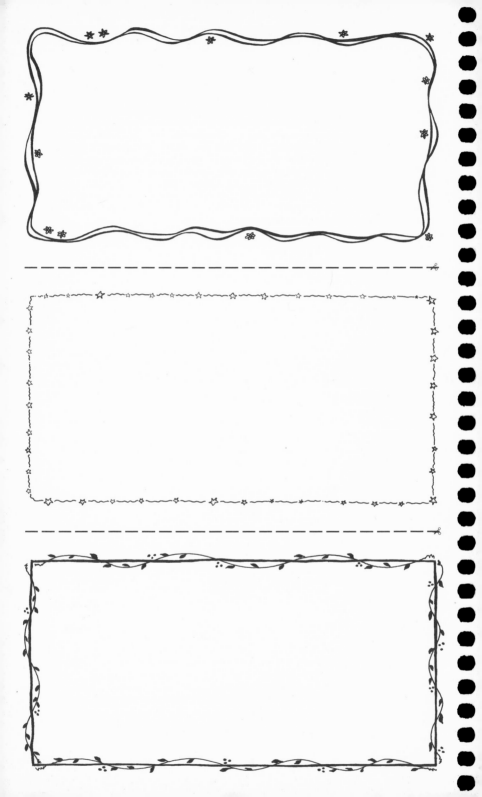